Dying To Live

Cycle C Sermons for Lent and Easter
Based on the Gospel Lessons

Charley Reeb

CSS Publishing Company, Inc.
Lima, Ohio

DYING TO LIVE

FIRST EDITION
Copyright © 2024
by CSS Publishing Co., Inc.

Library of Congress Cataloging-in-Publication Data

Names: Reeb, Charles D., 1973- author.
Title: Dying to live : cycle C sermons for Lent and Easter based on the
   gospel lessons / Charley Reeb.
Description: First edition. | Lima, Ohio : CSS Publishing Company, Inc.,
   [2024]
Identifiers: LCCN 2024031497 | ISBN 9780788031236 (paperback)
Subjects: LCSH: Lent--Prayers and devotions. | Lenten sermons. |
   Easter--Sermons. | Common lectionary (1992). Year C.
Classification: LCC BV85 .R454 2024 | DDC 242 / .34--dc23 / eng / 20240801
LC record available at https:/ /lccn.loc.gov /2024031497

For more information about CSS Publishing Company resources, visit our website at www.csspub.com, email us at csr@csspub.com, or call (800) 241-4056.

e-book:
ISBN-13: 978-0-7880-3124-3
ISBN-10: 0-7880-3124-4

ISBN-13: 978-0-7880-3123-6
ISBN-10: 0-7880-3123-6   PRINTED IN USA

To the loving people of the First UMC of Lakeland.

Contents

Ash Wednesday
Matthew 6:1-6;16-21

Jesus Said What?

I must confess that when I get up to preach, I find it fascinating that most of my listeners want to follow a man who was so radical and offensive that he was executed.

Will Willimon liked to tell about the time he preached on Jesus' parable "The Laborers in the Vineyard" (Matthew 20:1-16). After the service a young lady came up to him and said, "I was really troubled by the service today." She asked, "Where do you get these stories that you tell in your talk?" Willimon replied, "Stories? I guess I get them from growing up in South Carolina." She said, "Well I was really bothered by the one today. I just don't think that's anyway to treat people. I mean, if you work longer than other people, you should get paid more." Willimon said, "Wait a minute! That's not my story, that's from Matthew." She said, "Matthew?" He said, "Yeah, it is in the Bible." Willimon noticed that she was wearing an usher tag and he asked, "Why are you ushering here?" She replied, "Well that tall guy over there, I'm dating him. And he needed somebody to usher today so he called me and here I am."

Willimon said, "I am curious. What is your religious background?" She said, "We went to church some when I was a kid, but I'm not anything really." Willimon said, "We'll let me tell you something. Just for your information, there is a sense in which you are the only person who got the story this morning. You found it offensive to your notion of justice. Right? Outrageous. Right? Well, just so you know, the man who told that story was later murdered for telling it. You got it. It really is an offensive, outrageous story. You got it."

Mark Twain said it well for many people: "It is not what I don't understand in the Bible that troubles me; it is what is perfectly clear that does." Anybody who gives a serious reading of the gospels and what Jesus had to say can't help but appreciate Twain's remarks.

The church talks a lot about Jesus, but I have found that the church says very little about what Jesus taught. It doesn't take a biblical scholar to figure out why. Jesus' teachings are radical and often offensive to us, so we find it easier to talk about Jesus in general terms instead of the transforming gospel that he preached. In fact, the first time Jesus got up to preach in his hometown, he almost got killed. The people he grew up with were so offended they tried to throw him off a cliff! How's that for sermon feedback? Jesus had a knack for ticking people off.

In this message, we are going to take a look at the challenging and often radical things Jesus taught. Why did he say these things? And why do Jesus' teachings trouble us so much? If we find them so troubling, why do Jesus' words still have such an impact on us today?

There are perhaps no other words in the gospels that trouble us more than those we find in *The Sermon on the Mount* (Matthew 5-7): *"You have heard that it was said to the people long ago, 'You shall not murder, and anyone who murders will be subject to judgment.' But I tell you that anyone who is angry with a brother or sister will be subject to judgment. "You have heard that it was said, 'You shall not commit adultery.' But I tell you that anyone who looks at a woman lustfully has already committed adultery with her in his heart.*

All that would be tough enough to swallow but then Jesus drops this big one: *"You have heard that it was said, 'Eye for eye, and tooth for tooth.' But I tell you, do not resist an evil person. If anyone slaps you on the right cheek, turn to them the other cheek also. And if anyone wants to sue you and take your shirt, hand over your coat as well. If anyone forces you to go one mile, go with them two miles. Give to the one who asks you, and do not turn away from the one who wants to borrow from you. "You have heard that it was said, 'Love your neighbor and hate your enemy.' But I tell you, love your enemies and pray for those who persecute you, that you may be children of your Father in heaven. If you love those who love you, what reward will you get? Are not even the tax collectors doing that? And if you greet only your own people, what are you doing more than others? Do not even pagans do that? [48] Be perfect, therefore, as your heavenly Father is perfect."*

And then in our assigned text in chapter 6 of Matthew, we find these words of Jesus in verse 14 and 15: *"For if you forgive other people when they sin against you, your heavenly Father will also forgive you. But if you do not forgive others their sins, your Father will not forgive your sins."*

Jesus said what? Now, this is almost too much to bear, isn't it? Can you believe we claim to follow someone who tells us to turn the other cheek, forgive others, and love our enemies? It's outrageous, especially in our culture whose mantra is "Protect what's yours. Don't be a doormat."

The Jesus who told us he was the living water that satisfied our deepest thirst, we will take that Jesus. The Jesus who told us he would give us eternal life, we like that Jesus. But when Jesus commanded us to take it on the chin and not fight back and give to people we don't like and, horrors of horrors, to love our enemies and pray for those who persecute us and use us and gossip about us and slander us? Well, we would have none of that, thank you!

A colleague of mine tells about the time the dynamic preacher Tony Campolo came to preach at his church. He was so excited. Campolo is a fantastic preacher who can really motivate a congregation. He said for most of the sermon he had the congregation in the palm of his hand. They were agreeing with everything he said and hanging on his every word. They were loving him. Then the sermon turned and the energy went right out of the room. Why? Well, Campolo said an outrageous thing, a very offensive thing. He asked the congregation if they had prayed for Osama bin Laden (this was several years ago). Campolo reminded them that Jesus commanded us to pray for our enemies and that certainly included bin Laden. My colleague said he got angry letters for weeks about the outrageous thing Campolo said. It shouldn't surprise us. Jesus was murdered for what he said.

I remember calling up a close friend of mine to complain about someone I didn't particularly care for. I was upset and I was going on and on about why he had upset me, how I had been wronged and mistreated. My friend listened patiently. Then he said the most annoying thing in the world: "Have you prayed for him?" I don't know what I found more troubling — the fact that he asked the question or the fact that I had forgotten to pray for him.

Sometimes it is hard to follow Jesus. Why did Jesus have to say what he said? Why can't we just cluster together with people that we like and say, "good riddance" to those we don't care for? Why can't we feel good about how good we are and enjoy a little disdain for those who do all the bad things in this world? Well, the answer why gets to the heart of the gospel and why the Christian faith has stood the test of time. And sometimes that answer comes from the mouth of a child.

When my son was five, he and I liked to play the mobile version of Battleship. It is a fantastic game. It is not your childhood battleship! You use torpedo's, radar, bombs, and the like. It is an exciting game of strategy. One time, Paul and I were playing a person online and beating him over and over again. He kept playing us because I am sure he wanted to win. So, in the middle of a game, Paul grabbed the phone of out my hands and said, "Daddy, let's let him win this time." I was irate. "What in the world are you talking about? Give me my phone. No way!"

Then Paul looked at me and said, "But Daddy don't you get up and talk to people about being kind to others." Needless to say, I was convicted. He was right. But what I wanted to say was, "Yeah Paul, but not in Battleship!"

I think Jesus' words are so tough and challenging because he obliterates our boundaries of love. We are always trying to draw lines, noting where God's loves stops. Jesus is always erasing those lines. What's more is Jesus is always obliterating the values we feel good about. What we often think is good and noble does not come close to the values of God's kingdom.

We believe in the American dream — make as much money as you want and be free to do whatever you want. It's your life. It's your money. Eat, drink, and be merry! Yet Jesus rather inconveniently replies through the parable of the rich fool, "You fool! Right now your life is required of you and all this money, whose will it be? You never realized that God made you rich so you could bless others."

We believe in being fair, in giving people what they deserve. We believe in rewarding hard work. Yet Jesus inconveniently replies through the parable of the laborers in the vineyard, "I choose to pay those who worked one hour in the field the same amount as those who worked all day. Are you envious because I am generous?"

We believe God is going to reward us for being faithful to him all these years. Yet Christ turns to a lifetime criminal on the cross who wasn't faithful a day in his life and converted at the last minute and says, "You will be with me in paradise." That's not fair! A man on death row converts at the last minute and he gets the same reward as those of us who have been faithful our entire lives!

We believe in getting even! "He hurt me and I am going to hurt him back. What he did was unforgivable and inexcusable!" And yet Jesus inconveniently replies, "Love your enemies. Pray for those who persecute you. Turn the other cheek. Forgive seventy times seven."

We believe in being successful, in being happy, in going after what we want. And yet Jesus inconveniently says, "Unless you come and die and take up a cross and follow me you cannot be my disciples. Unless you lose your life for my sake you will never find true life. Unless you learn to sacrifice for the sake of another you will never understand what life is. Unless you live a life putting yourself second and others first, you will not experience life."

The homeless man on the street could get a job and find a place to live if he wanted to, right? It wouldn't do any good to help him, right? The young man in and out of juvenile detention centers — he makes his own choices, right? It is irrelevant that he didn't have a daddy growing up and his mother beat him, right? You can't be responsible for irresponsible people, right? And Jesus inconveniently replies in Matthew, "I was hungry and you gave me something to eat. I was thirsty and you gave me something to drink. I was naked and you clothed me. I was in prison and you visited me. When you did it to them, you did it to me."

No wonder Jesus was murdered. Jesus gave us a high definition picture of what it looks like for God's will to be done on earth as it is in heaven. And sometimes that picture is so unlike our values we have to look away. Oh, we like to make all kinds of caveats about it. "Well, Jesus was just telling a story. Jesus was just trying to make a point. Jesus really didn't mean that. Jesus was just exaggerating."

We can dress it up all we want but the truth is Jesus turned our world upside down because he turned our values upside down. When the world sees no value in those who are oppressed, God calls us to bring them justice. When the world wants revenge, God calls us to show mercy. When everyone else around us has compromised their integrity, God calls us to keep ours. When all the world wants to do is use its resources for more power, God calls us to use our resources to heal suffering. Quite often the world's values clash with God's values. And that's why Jesus' words are often so difficult to take.

You want to know why those who heard Jesus preach for the first time got so angry and wanted to kill him? Because he said that the love he came to bring to the world was for everyone, not just those on the inside. It was even for those they hated the most! They couldn't stand it and almost threw him off a cliff! They would have if Jesus hadn't found the exit quickly! You can look it up in Luke 4:16-30.

The great irony is that the thing that offends us about Jesus is the one and only thing that will heal this world and transform it. Because when you boil down everything Jesus taught us it is that God's love is limitless. It knows no bounds. It always loves. Always forgives. Never gives up on anyone. Isn't this what Christ demonstrated on the cross?

It was this love that saved us. And Christ calls us to embody that same sacrificial love and forgiveness in the world.

God never intended his boundaries to be less than the whole world. None of us have a monopoly on God's love. Someone once said, "It is impossible to love Christ without loving others and it is impossible to love others without moving nearer to Christ."

Chuck Colson was once counsel to the White House and the founder of Prison Fellowship. He told about the time he took a group of people into Indiana State Penitentiary to conduct a worship service with inmates on death row.

After the service, the visitors were checking out, doing the necessary protocol when visitors leave the prison. But Colson was concerned when he discovered that one of the visitors was missing. Colson hurried back to the cell block to find the lost visitor. He was sitting in a cell with one of the prisoners with his arm around his shoulder. Colson was angry. He shouted at the man, "Don't you realize you're violating our privileges here? When we're asked to leave, we should leave! You can cause trouble for us by lingering behind like this!"

The man looked up and said, "I'm sorry. This is James Brewer. He's sentenced to die. I'm Judge Clement. I'm the man who pronounced the sentence upon him. Forgive me for lingering behind, but we both needed some time to forgive each other."

Jesus is relentlessly in love with the world. And thank God for that love. Where would be without that love? And would you believe there is room in his arms for everyone. There is room. There is plenty of room.

Amen.

First Sunday in Lent
Luke 4:1-13

Overcoming Temptation

I once read about a TV executive who wanted to boost ratings, so he decided to issue a warning on one of his network's most popular shows. For a week he advertised his show with this warning: "Viewer Discretion Advised." When his colleague asked him what was different about this particular episode, he replied, "Nothing really. I just know that people will tune in to something they think they shouldn't be watching."

It is true what Oscar Wilde said: "The easiest way to get rid of temptation is to yield to it." And so it is. But at what cost?

There she was with her tax forms spread all over the dining room table. The kids were running around. She had struggled to make ends meet as a single parent. Temptation slithered in and says, "Go ahead. Cheat a little on your taxes. You deserve it. You have worked too hard for Uncle Sam to take more of your money."

His buddy sent him a link to a website. He knew it was one of those adult websites and he paused before he clicked on it. Temptation slithered in and said, "Oh, don't be such a prude. It is not going to hurt you. Most of your friends go to those sites anyway. You're just looking."

She had been sober for a year. Her old friends came into town and they all went out to dinner. They all ordered wine. Temptation slithered in and said, "Oh, go ahead, just have one. You don't want to disappoint the girls."

They had been working many late nights together. They both were married and had kids of their own, but they couldn't help but feel some attraction toward each other. Temptation slithered in and said, "Go ahead. Take her out to dinner. You have earned a good time together. It's only dinner."

Temptations are like belly buttons. We all have them. To deny we are tempted is to stick our heads into the sand. There is a spiritual battle going on inside each of us. We all have some sort of spiritual kryptonite that weakens us and threatens our faith. And our faith is strengthened or weakened by how we respond to temptation.

Temptation is as old as Adam and Eve. They were in complete paradise. Their world was perfect. They never got sick. They never got upset. All their emotional, physical, and spiritual needs were met. All was right with them, with their God, and with their world. All they had to do was stay away from the tree in the middle of the garden. All they had to do was not eat from this tree and their perfect life would never end. This didn't seem too much to ask.

But you know how it is — you always want what you cannot have. Adam and Eve were curious about this tree — it was forbidden! I am sure they stared at it, dreamed about how the fruit tasted, fantasized about how it would make them feel. Here they were in paradise and they wanted the one thing God told them they could not have. We know the rest of the story.

Why is this the first moral story in the Bible? Because much of the suffering and pain in life begins with temptation. We don't see it that way at the beginning. In the beginning temptation looks exciting, fun, and pleasurable. Otherwise, it would not be temptation. But sin always looks better before we do it than after we do it. When we choose to open that door, we find out how ugly, empty and painful sin can be.

How can we learn to resist it? How can we prevent moral and spiritual disaster in our lives? We can do that by learning how Jesus resisted temptation.

Jesus understood the subtle power of temptation. There was this false notion that he never felt the pull of temptation. Nothing could be further from the truth. Jesus was fully God, but he was also fully human. He battled the same temptations that every human being battles. But Jesus fought temptation and won. Jesus resisted and in the crucible of temptation he discovered the one thing that was his destiny as the Son of God — to bring the world back to God through sacrificial love. Nothing would deter Jesus from the cross. Love always wins.

Just as Jesus resisted temptation and won, so each of us can resist temptation and live a victorious life. Our passage in Luke gives us all we need to know to resist temptation.

Build Up Your Resistance To Temptation

Just like our bodies build up resistance to illness and disease, so our souls must build up resistance to temptation and sin. We build up this resistance from being nourished by the word of God.

Did you notice how Jesus resisted temptation each time the tempter came at him? He quoted scripture! Each of his responses was from Deuteronomy. Since childhood Jesus had built up a resistance to temptation.

Many people are victims of temptation because they have not built up resistance with the word of God. When was the last time you spent ten minutes reading the Bible?

I like the old legend about the Cherokee Indian sitting with his grandson and telling him about the two wolves that live inside every person. He said, "One wolf is bad and the other one is good. And they are fighting a battle inside every heart." The little boy thought for a moment and then asked, "Which one wins?" The Indian replied, "The one you feed."

Remember Who You Are

The tempter was very crafty with Jesus. He didn't tempt Jesus with a chocolate cake or a woman in a bikini. He tempted Jesus with the power he had. He tempted Jesus to misuse his power and identity for the wrong purposes. Jesus was able to resist because he remembered who he was. He knew at a deep level who God had called him to be.

Many are defeated by temptation because they forget who they are. They forget their values and drift away from their foundation. Life gets busy. There are deadlines. Other goals and ambitions come in. The call of the world gets louder.

There was a young couple who were very successful in their respective jobs. They wanted to move up the social ladder. They got busier at work. They stopped going to church largely because they started to throw parties at their home on the weekends. They were proud about all the important people who were coming to their house. One night a little too much wine was served and the jokes got a little raunchier and things got a little out of hand. The noise woke up their little daughter and she came down stairs in her night gown. She saw all of the plates and food and glasses. She said, "Oh, you are about to eat. Let me say the blessing. 'God is great; God is good, let us thank him for our food. Amen.'" Some of the guests squirmed and said, "Well, it is getting late. I guess we ought to be getting home." Later, as the parents were cleaning up the dishes, the wife looked at her husband and said, "What do we think we're doing?"

Consider What's On The Other Side Of Temptation

Jesus knew what was on the other side of temptation; lies and emptiness. The devil is a liar. Evil never provides what is promised. No matter how reasonable or good temptation sounds, it is always a mirage hiding complete darkness. Sin always looks better before we do it than after we do it.

I recall performing a wedding ceremony in Memphis many years ago. It was for a fraternity brother of mine. It was a lot of fun. It was held in a beautiful hotel and many of my college friends were there. The reception took place in this grand ballroom and we were all having a great time. Sometime during the evening one of the bridesmaids approached me. She was a friend from college. She said, "You see that beautiful woman over there? She really likes you." I thought she was joking, but apparently, she wasn't. I was very flattered but I had just started dating Brandy and was very happy. When the reception concluded many of us gathered in the hotel lobby. Some had too much to drink and were calling cabs. Others were headed back to their hotel rooms. The lady who apparently liked me approached me and asked me if I was available. She wasn't talking about a cup of coffee. I'll never forget that moment. I looked at her and said, "I am very flattered but I don't think it's a good idea. Why don't I call you a cab?"

When thinking about that encounter I often ask, "What if I had made a different choice? My life might be very different."

I'm going to give you something to say to yourself whenever you face temptation that will help you. No matter the situation, it will always cause you to make the right decision. In fact, you can apply this to any decision you have to make and it will help you. It is a question that Andy Stanley based an entire book on. Here is the question: *"What is the wisest thing to do?"* Whenever you face temptation, whenever you have a critical decision to make, ask, "What's the wisest thing to do?" If you allow that question to guide you, you can never go wrong. Just think of all the pain and destruction that could be prevented in all of our lives if we asked this question whenever we faced temptation.

I have never been to the greyhound dog races, but I have seen them on television. Here are these beautiful dogs with long legs, bred for speed, chasing a mechanical rabbit around a track. These dogs run themselves ragged chasing this rabbit. Well, what is unfortunate is that when the dogs get to the point that they can no longer race, the owners take out ads in the newspapers to see if anybody wants to adopt one for a pet. You can have them for about 200 dollars; otherwise, if no one takes them, the dogs are put to sleep.

Fred Craddock once visited a home that had an adopted racing dog. He was a big, spotted greyhound, and he was lying in the den. One of the kids was pulling on its tail, and an older kid was resting his head on the dog's stomach, using it for a pillow. The dog just seemed so happy. And, you know, Craddock looked down at the dog and said, "Are you still racing?"

The dog said, "No, no. I don't race anymore."

He said, "Do you miss the glitter and excitement of the track?" "No," the dog replied.

"Well, what was the matter? Did you get too old to race?"

"No, I still had some race in me."

"Well, what then? Did you not win?" he asked.

"I won over a million dollars for my owner."

"Well, what was it? Bad treatment?"

"Oh no" the dog said, "they treated us royally when we were racing."

"Did you get crippled?" "No." "Then why?" he said.

The dog said, "I quit."

"You quit?"

"Yes," the dog said. "I quit."

"Why did you quit?"

The dog said, "Well, I discovered that what I was chasing was not really a rabbit, and I quit." The dog looked at him and said, "All that running and running and running and running and what was I chasing? It wasn't even real" (Craddock, *The Cherry Log Sermons*).

When you quit chasing those things that aren't real, that are empty, you will find a Savior who has been chasing you. And, believe me, nothing is more real than the love he has for you.

Amen.

The Great Divide

Over the years I have made a lot of trips from Central Florida to Atlanta, Georgia. As a result, I have become very familiar with I-75 North and South! I can tell you the best Dairy Queen to stop at and where the cleanest rest areas are. And, without fail, I always seem to stop at the same Chick-fil-A in Valdosta, Georgia, for lunch without thinking about it.

I also know the billboard ads well. The interstate is saturated with them. You have seen them — they advertise everything from pecan logs to houses of ill repute.

I have also become familiar with ads that advertise churches and Christian radio stations. I remember one ad advertising a local church. There is a happy middle-class family smiling and laughing in bed, just having a good time. Next to the picture is the traditional fish insignia. And there is the slogan: "Safe for the Whole Family." There was another one for a Christian radio station that said, "Safe for the Little Ears." Right there in the middle of all the ads for bars and booze is a nice safe ad for the whole family.

Safety is important to us. We like to be safe. We like to be protected and we like to protect what is important to us. When I am aboard a plane, I always feel better when the flight attendant says over the speaker, "Your safety is our number one concern." When I leave to go on long trips, people tell me, "Drive safely." At our church, we go to great lengths to make sure your kids are safe. We do background checks and require training for anyone working with kids. We like to be safe.

We like our money to be safe. We go to the bank and like seeing the sticker "FDIC Insured." We like our cars to be safe. We like ads that tell us that our cars have a high safety rating. We like our country to be safe and we spend enormous amounts of dollars ensuring that America is safe. We feel safe when we see our troops in uniform salute, as if to say, "You won't get hurt. Not on my watch."

We like our relationships to be safe. Many go to conferences to learn how to think "Win/Win" as we negotiate with people. We want to make decisions that are safe for everyone.

And we do like our religion safe, too. Like the ad says, we like it safe for the whole family. We like a God that we can trust. We like a God who will protect us and those we love if we believe in him and pray to him. We like a God who promises to give us eternal salvation if we put our faith in him. Many of us are drawn to faith because of the safety we believe it provides for us now and later.

This is why it is more than a little troubling to read something that Jesus said. Some people wish it were not in the Bible. It does not make us feel very safe, at least not to those of us who follow Jesus. Jesus comes across as a fire and brimstone preacher instead of a meek and mild teacher from Galilee that we see in paintings. He announces that he has come to bring fire to the earth and can't wait until the fire is kindled. And maybe most troubling of all is his announcement, "You think I have come to bring peace on earth? No, I come to bring division." And then he goes on to describe what happens at some weddings I have been a part of — "father against son, mother against daughter, mother-in-law against daughter in law…" (Matthew 10:34-36).

This sounds worse than an Alabama/Georgia football game!

Who is the cause of all this division? Jesus! I must say this text is difficult to swallow. Jesus, the cause of division? Jesus, a home wrecker? We didn't sign up for division, did we? I mean, we follow Jesus and pray to Jesus to bring families together, to bring people together, to bring unity. We follow Jesus because we know it will make everything alright, don't we? We follow Jesus because it is safe. Following Jesus is safe, isn't it?

I remember getting a haircut some time ago. The lady cutting my hair was new to the store. She asked what I did. I told her I was a preacher. She said, "Oh, that's great. I'm a Christian too. I just love Jesus. Jesus has done so much in my life. It is all about Jesus." I was moved by her testimony. She went on and on so much about Jesus I thought about hiring her at the church and putting her in charge of evangelism. Well, a lady who had been working there for a while came up to us and said, "You need to quiet down the talk about Jesus. Customers don't like it. A customer called corporate a few weeks ago and complained about a worker talking about religion. Keep your voices low." I paid my money. The lady cutting my hair said, "Well, if I get fired for talking about Jesus, I guess I will be fired."

I walked out of there and got in my car. My haircutter was outside smoking a cigarette. I don't know what got into me. I rolled down my window and yelled, "Praise Jesus?" There were some people who looked at me like I was green and had come from Mars. Some gave me dirty looks.

Following Jesus is safe, isn't it? What's wrong with Jesus? Why wouldn't anybody like Jesus? Why would Jesus create such a disturbance? Jesus tells us to love one another. Jesus teaches us to treat each other like we would like to be treated. Jesus, is the one who welcomes children. Why would anybody not like Jesus? What's not to like about Jesus?

I asked that question a lot some years ago after grieving over the execution of Daniel Terry. He was one of the ten humanitarian workers executed in Afghanistan. He and his wife were missionaries supported by a church I used to serve. He and I became friends. I shared a meal with him shortly before he was killed. We talked about Jesus. We talked about the love of Jesus, what it means to follow him. We talked about how Jesus called him to help people. And you know why he was executed? Because he was associated with Jesus. Now, can you believe that? Why wouldn't anybody like Jesus? Why would Jesus cause such anger, violence and division?

Well, I guess we shouldn't be surprised. Jesus warned us: "Don't think I have come to bring peace, but division!" He warned us that he would bring all kinds of division. Well, I guess we know it says that, but it is just hard for us to swallow it. It is just so hard to believe that Jesus would be the cause of such division. We want everyone to love Jesus and follow Jesus. We want the whole world to hold hands and sing about Jesus. Division?

I remember going to a passion play one time. It was a drama that reenacted the life and ministry of Jesus. It was well done. I sat next to a little girl and her dad. We all sat mesmerized by the play. The life of Jesus unfolded on the stage, the birth and the angels, the teachings, the miracles, the betrayal, the crucifixion, the resurrection. We left the play. The dad and the little girl were holding hands crossing the street. He said, "Did you like it, sweetie?" She replied, "Yeah, yeah, I did, daddy. But I didn't understand something, dad. Why did they have to kill him, daddy?" I thought he was going to say, "Well, see honey, he died for our sins." And he would have been right if he had said that. But he said something to her that was just as right. He said, "Well sweetie. They killed him because he made people feel uncomfortable. Sweetie, sometimes people don't like to hear the truth."

He was right. Jesus did make people feel uncomfortable. When you go around as God's son, filled with all kinds of truth and preaching it, it does make people upset. It does make some folks feel uncomfortable. It does cause division. Remember that time when that man came to Jesus and asked Jesus what he needed to do to have eternal life. Jesus saw his heart and said, "Sell everything you have and follow me." Jesus knew the man had a weakness for money and material things. And the Bible says the man went away sorrowful.

Remember that time when Nicodemus came to Jesus at night. Jesus saw his heart and said, "Nicodemus, you must be born from above. Nicodemus, you must change." Now, we don't know whether or not he did.

Remember that time Jesus approached the religious leaders and called out their hypocrisy and vanity. He called them "white washed tombs!" All clean on the outside and dirty on the inside.

Remember that time Jesus went into the temple. He saw the racket the religious leaders had going on. It was a good system in the temple, fleecing the people, taking advantage of them. Jesus ripped through the temple, turned over tables and screamed, "You have turned my Father's house into a den of thieves!"

You don't go around doing that without causing some division. You don't go around sharing the truth without making enemies. Try walking into an executive meeting of a Fortune 500 company and saying, "What does it profit you if you gain the whole world but lose your soul?" See how popular that makes you. Try walking into a bar and getting in the middle of a bar fight and saying, "Come on guys, turn the other cheek. Love each other. Pray for each other." See how popular that makes you. Try bringing home a bunch of homeless people and saying, "Honey, we have guests. Jesus said that if we do unto the least of these, we do it to him." See how popular that makes you.

I guess following Jesus is not so safe, is it? We forget that Jesus was very radical and controversial. We forget that Jesus was executed for what he said and did. And here we are willingly worshipping him, saying we want to follow him when we know it leads to a cross?

Our scripture passage is the Transfiguration. It is found in Luke 9. The whole text is about a misunderstanding. Peter, James and John go up a mountain with Jesus. They watch as Jesus is transfigured and Moses and Elijah appear. The three disciples completely miss the meaning of the event. They want to stay on the mountain with Jesus and bathe in the warmth and glory of that event. What they missed is that the Transfiguration was a confirmation of Jesus' upcoming death. Jesus was headed to a cross. Were Peter, James, and John ready to face a cross too?

This is what is so radical and divisive about Jesus. His love for us is so relentless that he doesn't just want an hour on Sunday morning. He doesn't just want a few dollars thrown into a plate. He doesn't just want a prayer here and there. He wants our entire lives. The most divisive thing about Jesus is that he does not want admirers; he wants followers. He does not want church members; he wants disciples. He doesn't want apologies; he wants repentance. He doesn't want respect; he wants allegiance. And you know why he wants so much and demands so much? Because he knows that unless we lose our lives in him, we will never find out what life is really all about.

But I'll warn you. If you decide to follow Jesus and do what he wants you to do and go where he wants you to go, don't be surprised if it puts you at odds with those that you love and those that you work with. Don't be surprised if it doesn't make you the most popular person in your neighborhood and community. For the world does not like to hear the truth. The world does not like the status quo disturbed. The world does not like its comfortable and convenient systems disrupted. Jesus said so.

I'll warn you. Sooner or later, each of us will have to make the choice between what is convenient, comfortable, popular, and what Jesus is calling us to do. And it will not be easy. It will not be safe. But it will be right and it will be true.

When Bishop Will Willimon was the minister at Duke Chapel he received a phone call from a very upset parent. The father was upset because his graduate school bound daughter had just told him she was going to 'throw it all away', as he put it, and go to do mission work in Haiti.

The father said, "This is absurd. She has a degree in mechanical engineering from Duke and she's going to dig ditches Haiti. I hold you personally responsible for this."

Willimon replied, "Me? What have I done?"

Father said, "Well, you filled her head with all that religious stuff. She thinks a lot of you. That's why she's doing this foolishness."

Willimon replied, "Now look, mister. Hold on. Didn't you have her baptized as a kid? Didn't you read her Bible stories and take her to Sunday school? Didn't you let her go on all those youth retreats and ski trips?"

The father said, "Well, yes..."

Willimon said, "Then it's *your* fault she believed all that stuff. Not mine. *You're* the one that introduced her to Jesus, not me."

The father replied, "But we never expected it to come to this. We never dreamed she would go to Haiti. We just wanted her to grow up to be a good Methodist."

Let those who have ears to hear, hear.

Amen.

Why Did God Allow That To Happen?

Have you ever wondered why bad things happen to good people? Have you ever asked, "If there is a God why do people suffer?" The world of theology calls it the theodicy question. The underlying angst of the question is this: If God can't stop suffering, then he is not great. If God can stop suffering and doesn't, then he is not good. So if God is great and good, then why is there suffering in the world? Why does he allow all this best bad stuff to happen?

The theodicy question is one of the biggest reasons why so many people choose not to believe in God. It is a huge roadblock to faith.

In fact, you may struggle with it. Maybe you have experienced unspeakable pain and tragedy in your life and the suffering you have been through keeps you from believing that a good, loving God exists. Or perhaps you have friends and relatives who have experienced great suffering and the theodicy question has kept them from going to church and believing in God. Maybe you believe in God but the theodicy question has lingered within you for a long time and at times it causes you to struggle with your faith.

You can take comfort from the fact that the theodicy question can be seen throughout the Bible. The Psalms ask it. Job asks it. Lamentations is full of it. The prophet Habakkuk complains to God about it. The prophet Jeremiah questions God about it: Why do the wicked prosper and the innocent suffer? Look at what Jeremiah says to God in the chapter 12, verse one:

> *"Righteous are you, O Lord, when I complain to you; yet I would plead my case before you. Why does the way of the wicked prosper? Why do all who are treacherous thrive?"*

Many of the biblical writers cry out with this same burning question that we ask today. So don't be afraid to express your anger and complaints to God. It seems like half of the Old Testament is filled with complaints against God. There is more faith in complaining to God than there is in being silent. And quite often a season of anger and complaint will lead to a deeper understanding of God and faith.

But what is the answer to Jeremiah's complaint and our complaint?

Let me begin by mentioning that one of the biggest problems with this question is how some people answer it. In fact, the way many Christians answer the question of suffering is not only unhelpful but harmful.

A popular way folks respond to the theodicy question is "Everything happens for a reason." How many of you have heard that one? Usually this platitude is said in the context of difficulty or adversity. We get bad news. We are disappointed. Life takes a bad turn and we have a well-meaning friend say to us, "Everything happens for a reason." Now, this phrase comes in other forms: "God must be testing you" or "It must be God's will" or "Things don't happen to you; they happen for you."

All of these religious phrases could fall under the heading of "Everything happens for a reason." And they all mean that your trial, difficulty, bad news, problem, or adversity was planned by a higher power, the universe or God. It was supposed to happen to you. There is a larger reason why it happened to you. It was intentional. When Christians say it, they mean God orchestrated or planned your adversity for a purpose. God has predetermined everything. We are the puppets and God is manipulating the strings. We just go by the script. Everything that happens, even tragedy and difficulty, has been scripted by God.

I guess some people are comforted by what this platitude implies, but do we really believe that God has orchestrated all the pain and tragedy in our lives? Do we really believe that God plotted 9/11 for a purpose like testing our country? Do we really believe that public shootings happen for a reason? Do we really believe that God is behind the bloodshed and tragedy in the world? Do we really believe that God intentionally plots suffering to see if we can pass a test? And if we do believe all this, what does it say about the God we believe in?

I recall doing a funeral for a man in another church I served. After the funeral I attended a reception at the family's home. I was having refreshments in the living room with some of the family of the deceased. Sitting next to me was a middle-aged woman who was a member of the family. I didn't know her. I had just met her that day. She was a very honest person. She looked at me and said, "I'm not a big fan of ministers." I smiled and said, "Me, either. I have a problem with many ministers as well." I asked, "So, why do you have issues with ministers?" I was not prepared for what she said. Under normal circumstances I don't think she would have been so forthcoming but grief can instill liberating honesty. She said, "When I was in my twenties my mother died of cancer. It was devastating because I was very close with my mother. At the time, I had a friend who was a strong Christian tell me that "everything happens for a reason." She said that I needed to accept this as God's will and move on. When she said that I decided I would never have anything to do with God, religion, or the church."

I did my best to explain to her how wrong and insensitive her friend's remarks were but the spiritual damage had been done. Did her friend have good intentions? Sure. Was she just trying to be comforting? Sure. But the religious platitude presented God as someone who planned that tragedy in her life and she wanted nothing to do with a God like that. I can't blame her.

When I was in seminary one of my best friends in college was killed by a drunk driver. He and his girlfriend were on bikes in Austin, Texas, on their way to the hill country for the afternoon. In my friend's pocket was an engagement ring. He was going to propose marriage to her that day. That proposal never happened. A drunk driver struck both of them, killing my friend instantly. His girlfriend suffered multiple injuries and was in a coma for two months.

I was invited by my friend's family to read scripture and speak at the funeral. I remember going to the viewing the day before the funeral. It was an open casket. I recall looking at my friend in the casket and someone standing next to me saying something I will never forget. I don't know who the person was, but he looked at my friend in the casket and said, "It is hard to understand God's will sometimes." Now, I was ready to give that man a good sermon, but it wasn't the time or place. I thought to myself, "God didn't do this! A drunk driver did!"

But we have all heard the language. It is amazing how some Christians will blame suffering on God. A baby dies and someone says, "God needed another angel in heaven." A young mother dies of breast cancer leaving a husband and two kids behind and someone says, "God works in mysterious ways." A group of teenagers on their way to prom are killed in a car accident and someone says, "God must have had a purpose." We get bad news. We are disappointed. Life takes a bad turn and we have a well-meaning friend say to us, "Everything happens for a reason." She received news from the doctor that she has cancer and her friend says, "God never gives you more than you can handle."

However, it doesn't help the cause of the Christian faith that we have particular Christian personalities say dreadful things on television. Some of you will remember that after 9/11 a well-known religious figure appeared on TV and told the world that God orchestrated 9/11 to punish America for its sins. We wonder why some folks are turned off by Christians and the church. And then we wonder why some folks don't want to have anything to do with God? Why would they when they hear Christians say that God causes great suffering and pain in the world? Why would they want to believe in a God like that? I don't believe in a God like that.

Neither did Jesus. In our assigned passage in Luke 13 Jesus is asked about a great tragedy and if God was to blame. Jesus was quick to say no.

Bottom line — everything does not happen for a reason, at least not in the way people usually mean it. The God I know and love would not plot and plan suffering or tragedy. Sometimes things happen because of the foolishness of others. Sometimes things happen because of our own bad choices. Sometimes bad things happen because we live in an evil and imperfect world. But let's not blame tragedy and suffering on God.

Why does God allow bad things to happen? When God created us, he gave us free will. He loves us enough to allow us to choose to love him back. Otherwise, we would be a bunch of robots programmed to love and there is really no such thing as forced love. If God took away our freedom to do evil God would also be taking away our freedom to do good. But the shadow side to our freedom is that there is room for bad choices, mistakes, bad timing and decisions, all of which can cause pain, difficulty, frustration, tragedy and adversity. But when bad things happen it doesn't mean God caused them to happen.

If God is not behind our tragedy and difficulty, then how do we deal with it? How do we make sense of it? If God is great and good, then why do we suffer? As Christians we have the assurance that one day Christ will come in glory and all of our questions will be answered, all of the great mysteries will be solved, all of our confusion will turn into clarity, and every tear will be wiped away. But until that great day comes, we have to cope with suffering in life. So if God does not cause tragedy and suffering, what role does God play in suffering? Where is God when it hurts? Where is God when planes crash and earthquakes come and people die in car accidents? Where is God and is he involved at all? How do we make sense of suffering if we follow a loving and powerful God?

I want to offer some things that have helped me as I have struggled with the theodicy question. My prayer is that they will help you too.

First, I want to lift up a passage of scripture that tells us exactly where God is when we suffer. It comes from the Old Testament, from the prophet Isaiah. Isaiah was prophesying about Jesus and he said something that I think all of us need to remember when it comes to our own suffering. In fact, what I am about to read may bring healing to you today. Isaiah 53:3-4:

> *"He was despised and rejected by men, a man of sorrows and familiar with suffering. Like one from whom men hide their faces he was despised and we esteemed him not. Surely, he took up our infirmities and carried our sorrows."*

Did you see that? He carried our sorrows. He carries our sorrows.

I want you to hear that today. Wherever you are, whatever you are going through, whatever pain you are in God carries your sorrows. He shares it with you. He cries with you. He aches with you. He loves you too much for you to deal with it alone. Romans 8 reminds us that nothing shall separate us from God's love. You see, Jesus' death tells us that when we suffer, God suffers with us. The cross and resurrection reveal that God experiences our suffering and has the power to redeem it.

But there is another thing I want you to remember when you struggle with the question of God and suffering. Harry Emerson Fosdick once said, "Goodness is a far greater problem for the atheist than evil is for the believer." Instead of focusing on the evil and suffering in the world, look at all the goodness that abounds! Where does all this goodness come from? It can only come from a loving God who cares for us.

Allow the goodness in the world to lead you back to the goodness of God. And may the goodness of God lead you to help heal the suffering in the world. God wants to heal suffering in this world, and you know how he is going to do it? Through you and through me!

When God wants something done in this world, he counts on his church to do it!

You want to see God at work in the midst of suffering, just open your eyes. He works through people all the time. And he wants to work through you!

A few years ago a brain surgeon in Birmingham, Alabama, walked six miles through a blizzard to save a patient's life. His name was Dr. Zenko Hyrnkiw. He was a neurosurgeon at Trinity Medical Center. He had just finished surgery at a neighboring hospital when someone called him to get to Trinity ASAP for an emergency surgery. He tried to drive there, but there were roadblocks and snow everywhere. The hospital called him again. He said, "I'm not getting anywhere. I'm walking."

It took Dr. Zenko about five hours to get to Trinity. At around 12:30pm he walked in and the patient had already been prepped for surgery. He spoke to the patient's family and off to the OR he went. As of Thursday morning, that patient was stable. The head nurse told reporters that without the surgery the patient would have died. When Dr. Zenko was questioned about it, he replied, "I'm just doing my job."

What if Christians just did their job? A lot of suffering in this world would be alleviated. What is our job as Christians? To help God alleviate suffering in the world. So often we complain to God and wonder why he is not doing something about the suffering in the world. I'm sure his reply is, "I was going to ask you the same thing! I am trying to do something, through you! You are my hands and feet in this world!"

I believe the best help I can give as we grapple with the question of why bad things happen to good people is to offer another question: What happens to good people when bad things happen to them? This is a question that the Bible clearly answers.

In the eighth chapter of Romans, Paul used several words to describe the pain and suffering of life: hardship, persecution, distress, nakedness, peril, the sword. Paul and the early Christians were very much in touch with unfair suffering. But what did Paul say happens to us when we experience bad things? Not only did he say that we will never be separated from God's love, but in Romans 8:28 Paul says something truly remarkable:

> "All things work together for good for those who love God, who are called according to his purpose."

Wow! Paul put it another way: *"We are more than conquerors through him who loved us."*

This means that evil and pain are never the will of God, but God can take evil and pain and use it for good. Over and over again in life we see this. When evil attacks with pain, God uses it to build character. When evil shows resistance, God uses it to build strength. When evil cripples with tragedy, God finds a way to victory. When evil destroys with death, God restores life. God is in the transformation business. God can turn our trouble into triumph! The worst thing is never the last thing.

The ultimate example of this is Jesus' work on the cross. Before Jesus, the cross represented suffering, shame, punishment, and death. But he came and transformed it into a symbol of victory, forgiveness, love and life. So whenever we gaze upon the cross, we are reminded that God can take what is ugly and make it beautiful.

Here is today's message. It is a powerful statement I found some time ago. I'm unsure of its source, but it is very helpful: *"Everything that happens to you is not God's will but God has a will in everything that happens to you."* And God's will is to turn your trouble into triumph. You don't have to be a victim in life! You can walk in confidence in the Lord. You can say, "I don't know what this day is going to bring, but I know that God will bring me through it. I know that there is nothing I am going to face that God and I can't handle. I know by the power of God I will be more than a conqueror!"

How do you become "more than a conqueror" for God? What is the first step? Pray, "Lord, I hand my pain over to you. You take it and use it for your purposes and glory. Use it in whatever way you want to use it, Lord. It is yours. Do with it what you will." You may want to keep a journal and mark the day you gave your difficulty to God. Keep track of it and you may be amazed one day how God used it for good!

My friend Andrew's funeral that I mentioned earlier was an ugly experience but God did do something beautiful with it. The night before the funeral I was talking with one of Andrew's childhood friends. We were sitting on a dock looking out at a lake. He confessed that he was not very "religious." He asked, "So, you're a minister huh?" I said, "Yes, I am." He asked, "How do you deal with death and funerals? How do you get through them? That's got to be tough?" I said, "Yeah, it is. But God gives me the strength to be able to minister in those situations. It is never easy but God helps me." He replied, "You really believe all that stuff?" I said, "I sure do. With all my heart."

The next day at the funeral I read some scripture and said a few words about Andrew. After the funeral Andrew's friend approached me and said, "This faith stuff is real to you, isn't it?" I said, "It sure is." Then he said, "I've never read the Bible very much. Could you recommend a translation I should read?" I said, "Here, take mine. It's yours." It was my favorite Bible. I loved that Bible. But a year later I heard that he was a Christian and active in a church! Now, every time I miss my favorite Bible I think of how God took what was ugly and made it beautiful.

The message I want to leave you with is that God can take what is ugly in your life and make it beautiful. If you're patient enough and open to what God wants to do in your life, God will turn your trouble into triumph.

Amen.

Fourth Sunday in Lent
Luke 15:1-3, 11b-32

You Can Go Home Again

What is God really like? This is a very important question because everyone's faith is based on what they think God is like. Some people behave as if God is a mean judge trying to catch us in the act and therefore their whole life is about running from God or following strict rules all the time. Some people think God is a heavenly accountant who tallies good points and bad points and at the end of our lives he will punish us or reward us depending upon which points are higher. Some think God is some distant being who made the world and put it in motion but this God has better things to do than be involved with humanity.

But what is God really like? Maybe you have been struggling with that question your whole life. Maybe you have never really liked religion and church because you were brought up in a way that presented God as boring, mean and judgmental. Maybe you have always thought there was a higher power or being that created the world, and you have given a lot of thought about God, but you are just not sure what this God is like. Should you be afraid of God? Should you bother God? What does God want from you?

Maybe you are carrying around a lot of guilt and you really want to know what God thinks of you and what you have done. Maybe you have gone to church occasionally or maybe you have been in church your whole life and you've heard mixed messages about what God is like. You wonder if anyone can give you a clear answer.

Back in Jesus' day, people had the same burning question. That is why crowds of people gathered to hear Jesus speak and ask him questions. Jesus said and did some profound things in order to show us what God is like. One of the most profound things he did was tell the parable of the prodigal son.

The Bible does not get any better than in Luke 15 where we read the parable of lost sheep, lost coin, and the lost or prodigal son. In many ways, the parable of the prodigal son is one of the greatest stories ever told, not just in the Bible, but in the history of literature. Movies, songs, poems, books, and novels throughout the ages have been based on this powerful story. And the parable is only twenty verses long! People who don't consider themselves religious know and love this parable. Over and over again, folks from all walks of life have been drawn to this parable.

Why do people love it so much? Why are so many drawn to it? Why is it so intriguing? Because it answers the burning question we all have. It tells us what God is like.

I want us to take a closer look at this parable today because if you have wondered what God is like this parable is for you. If you are ever in doubt about what God is like look no further than this parable.

The father in the story is God. Be sure you watch the father in the parable. The father had two sons. The younger one said, "I know it all. Life would be so much more fun if I could get out of dodge, leave this life and do what I want. Dad, give me my inheritance early. I want to be on my own." The father gave him the money and he left his father, left his home, ran off and did what he wanted to do.

Adam Hamilton wisely noted that in this parable the young son thought life would be better without his father. He wanted the blessings and gifts of the father without a relationship with the father.

Have you ever been in a situation in your life where people cared more about what you could give, what you could offer, than about you or having a relationship with you? Maybe it was a friend or co-worker. How did it make you feel? All they wanted was money or some connection you had with another person or some resource you could offer but they really didn't care about you. They never wanted to spend time with you. It was all about what you could for them. You felt used and unappreciated.

Hamilton believed God feels the same way when we take his gifts and blessings and enjoy the life he has given us without appreciating him and developing a relationship with him. I think that is one of the things Jesus is trying to tell us in this parable. God wants a relationship with us. God wants to be in our lives. He wants to love on us, guide us, connect with us, give us a purpose, listen to us and he wants us to listen to him. But here is the thing — God will not force a relationship on us. He gives us freedom to choose.

Notice the father in the parable. He didn't stop his son from taking the money and running. As painful as it was for the father not to stop him, he let him go because love can't be forced.

So, the young son went off to Las Vegas and had a good ole time! "I'm free! I'm free! I can do what I want. I have all this money. There is no limit to what I can do. I have no one telling me what to do. Let's party!"

Soon that party was over. The son hit rock bottom. He ran out of money and found himself working with pigs, craving the food they ate. Remember, he was Jewish. Pigs were considered unclean to him, yet he was living and working in pig slop. That was about as low as he could get! Life without his father was not as exciting as he thought it was going to be. Sitting in pig slop, feeling tired, cold and hungry, the reality of being away from his father did not match the picture in his mind.

Sin always looks better before we do it than after we do it, doesn't it? Running away from God always seems more exciting than it really is. Life without God never delivers what it promises.

I remember when I was about eight or nine, I ran away from home. I thought it would be so nice to be on my own — no one telling me what to do, when to go to bed, and what to eat. I packed a backpack with toys, a sandwich, and snacks. I threw a folder in the pack that had paper for me to draw on. I ran down to a creek, sat on a rock, and ate my sandwich. It felt great! Then I pulled out my folder filled with drawing paper and a picture of my parents fell out. I had used it for a project at school. I remember looking at the picture and thinking about how much I loved my parents. Suddenly, I became terrified of what it would be like without them. I quickly packed up my things and ran home! I ran into the kitchen and hugged my mom. I looked at the clock and I had not been gone more than thirty minutes! They didn't even miss me!

Sooner or later in life, all of us come to the place where we realize we need more than the things of this world. We need God. We need more than life. We need the creator of life. We need more than money and power. We need love and relationship. Those in AA call it a moment of clarity. Some call it a conversion experience. More traditional folks call it being born again. But it is all the same experience — it is getting to the place in your life when success doesn't satisfy anymore, power doesn't satisfy anymore, money and things don't satisfy anymore, constant adventures of play and travel don't satisfy anymore, and you feel a hunger deep in your soul for the only thing that will satisfy — the unconditional love and companionship of the Father! Jesus put it this way in the context of the parable: "He came to himself." The younger son came to the realization that his life was empty without his father.

You might be in the same place today. You realize how empty your life has become without God in it. You have been chasing one empty promise after the other, thinking it will be enough, but it always leaves you cold. There is not enough sexual pleasure, money, power or prestige that can satisfy, that can do what a relationship with the heavenly Father can do in your life.

The younger son came to this realization. Let's read what he did next:

> But when he came to himself, he said, 'How many of my father's hired hands have bread enough and to spare, but here I am dying of hunger! I will get up and go to my father, and I will say to him, "Father, I have sinned against heaven and before you; I am no longer worthy to be called your son; treat me like one of your hired hands."

This is how desperate the young son had become! This is how empty he was. He wanted to go home and be a paid servant for his father instead of remaining where he was on his own. He wasn't expecting to be accepted and loved back into the family. He wasn't expecting to be called a son. In fact, in Jesus' day, a son who did what the younger son did would have been disowned by his father, cut off from the family. But he was so empty, so miserable, so desperate for his father that he just wanted to be considered a hired hand for his father. That's it.

I know so many people who delay coming back to God because they think just like the younger son. They think they have wandered away so far, screwed up so badly, that the best they can hope for is to be a slave to God. They think that if they come back to God they will have to fulfill some ridiculous religious duty and God will punish them and remind them of what they did and keep tabs on them and maybe they will get into heaven. Perhaps that is where some of you are today. You think if you come back home to God you are going to feel worse about what you have done and where you have been. You think God will never let you forget what you did.

Is that what you think God is like? Think again. Let's allow Jesus to tell us what God is like:

> *So he set off and went to his father. But while he was still far off, his father saw him and was filled with compassion; he ran and put his arms around him and kissed him.*

Did you see what the father did? It says when his son was far off, he saw him! This means the father had been looking for him! Every day the father had looked anxiously down the driveway hoping his son would return. Every day the father had looked outside the kitchen window waiting for his son — waiting and hoping.

Then the text says that when the father finally saw his son he ran after him! Fathers in Jesus' day didn't run for anything. It was considered undignified and shameful. Yet, Jesus said the father ran after him! When he got to his son, he didn't lecture him. He threw his arms around his son and kissed him.

The son then began his apology speech, but notice what happens when he starts apologizing:

> *Then the son said to him, 'Father, I have sinned against heaven and before you; I am no longer worthy to be called your son.' But the father said to his slaves, 'Quickly, bring out a robe—the best one—and put it on him; put a ring on his finger and sandals on his feet. And get the fatted calf and kill it, and let us eat and celebrate; for this son of mine was dead and is alive again; he was lost and is found!' And they began to celebrate.*

Did you see that? As the son was apologizing, his father interrupted him — "Forget all that. Call the DJ! Call the caterer! Call our neighbors and friends! We are going to have a party! We are going to celebrate! My son is home!"

What is God like? God is your loving creator who relentlessly loves you and will never stop loving you. Our God is a God of love who always welcomes you home. This is what Jesus taught and more importantly what he embodied.

Here is Jesus' invitation for each of us today:

> *"If you are tired from carrying heavy burdens, come to me and I will give you rest." — Matthew 11:28 (CEV)*

Regardless of what you've heard, Christianity is not a religion; it is a relationship. It is not something that confines you; it is something that sets you free. It is not something that shames you; it is something that empowers you.

I don't know what you think of God. I don't know what kind of religious upbringing you had. But one thing I do know is God loves you and God doesn't want to put any more burdens on you. In fact, God wants to take them away and give you love, hope, peace and joy. This parable proves it. It came from the lips of Jesus.

Perhaps you are thinking, "But Charley, you don't know what I have done. You don't know how dark I feel. You don't know how lost I am." Well, let me tell you a true story.

Reverend Dr. Riley Short is one of my mentors. I was his associate pastor for four years at First UMC of Lakeland, Florida. He loved to tell the story of the time he was a young pastor with young kids. It had been a tough week at the church. He was late getting to his sermon and was toiling in his study at home on a Saturday afternoon. One of his young daughters barged into his study and said, "Daddy, Daddy, look at the picture I drew!" Riley got angry and said, "What do you think you are doing? I've told you a hundred times to always knock before you come in! Daddy is working on a sermon and can't talk to you right now. Get out of here and go play." She left in tears with the picture in her hands.

Riley went back to his desk and tried to finish his sermon, but inspiration would not come. He was stuck. Then he sensed God say to him, "You think you are so important, working on a sermon. People won't remember that sermon five minutes after you preach it. But you just broke your little girl's heart. You need to do something about it."

Riley opened his study door and called his daughter to come in. She came in sheepishly still holding her picture. Riley said, "Sweetheart, I am not mad at you. I want to tell you something. Come sit on my lap. I am so sorry I got angry at you. I love you with all my heart. You are more important than a sermon. Can you forgive me?" "Of course Daddy" she replied. Then Riley said, "Now, show me the picture you drew." She said, "I drew our house. See, there is grass. There are the windows, and here is our dog sitting on the porch." "Oh, I love it!" Riley said.

Riley then looked at his daughter and said, "Sweetheart, Daddy is working on his sermon and is stuck. I need your help. I am talking about Jesus tomorrow. If you could tell the world anything about Jesus, what would you say?" She thought for a moment and said, "I would say…if you ever get lost, Jesus will find you."

You are never really lost. Jesus knows where you are and is always ready to reach out to you and pick you up, shower you with love and grace and make you new again. So come home. It's time to come home.

Amen.

Finding God

Where have you seen God in your life? We believe as Christians that God is intimately connected to us and to our world, so therefore God should show himself in some fashion, in some form. So where have you seen God or where do you see God? Many people believe that they can see God through signs and wonders and miracles, and certainly that's very biblical. It's like the guy who, believed that the face of Jesus was in the bird droppings on his windshield. He truly felt Jesus was actually looking at him. Or what about that man who was also in the news who said he felt Jesus was looking at him through his burnt breakfast burrito? What about that little boy in South Carolina who caught a stingray and said he believed the face of Jesus was on the belly of that stingray? Of course, there was that famous man who claimed to see the face of Jesus on his Walmart receipt.

While I don't doubt the God can and does make himself known in these ways, I believe we often look too hard for God. I believe God reveals himself in much simpler, pedestrian ways, which is why we often we miss God. Maybe you're trying desperately to find God — to see God in some way and you've been disappointed. Maybe you've asked God to give you some sign that you're going in the right direction and you just have not seen God in your burnt burritos!

Perhaps you just want to know that God exists but you haven't really seen any sign from God in the sky. God has not revealed himself to you, and you are very frustrated about it. Again, you are probably looking too hard for God.

I want to share a text of scripture with you that I believe shows us that God often reveals himself to us in ordinary ways. Usually God is right under our noses, which is why we often miss God because it's the last place we think to look. I'm talking about a particular experience of Jesus when he was having dinner at Lazarus' house. In this very text of scripture, we see how God often reveals himself to us.

Mary took a very costly ointment of nard, broke open the jar and poured the ointment on his head. Now, back in Jesus' day, it was a very common custom and ritual for the host of the house to put a drop of perfume on the guests' head. Back then, people didn't bathe very much so I'm sure it was very welcome. And yet, here was this woman at this party. We don't know who she was, we don't know where she came from, we just know what was in her heart. She took this expensive bottle of perfume, and she didn't just put a drop on Jesus' head, she broke open the entire jar and she poured it on Jesus' head. Jesus' head and his hair was drenched with this perfume, and the whole room smelled like this beautiful perfume. It just permeated the entire room. Jesus was constantly doing kind things for people, and finally someone was doing something kind for him.

But Judas thought Mary was being wasteful. He said, *"Why was this ointment wasted in this way? For this ointment could have been sold for more than three hundred denarii and the money given to the poor."* But Jesus was quick to rebuke Judas and told him she was preparing him for burial.

Mary had an impulse to love and she acted upon it. I believe God used her impulse to love to encourage Jesus as he faced the cross. I believe God used that woman's lovely act to give Jesus the courage to face the cross.

What does this story have to do with finding God? It has everything to do with it. Here is the message, plain and simple, God is found whenever and wherever the impulse to love is acted upon.

Whenever you are the recipient of something lovely, beautiful and kind when you need it the most, that is God. The letter that you received that gave you the kind of encouragement you so desperately needed? That was God. The person who squeezed your hand when you felt so lonely? That was God. The friend who listened to you, who really cared and genuinely loved you? That was God. The story that you read that tightened your throat and inspired you? That was God.

It's impossible to get close to God without getting closer to other people. That's just good theology. The Bible says we can't say we love God and hate our brother. The closer we get to the Lord the closer he draws us to those in need.

God is so intimately connected to each one of his children, that whenever God wants to connect with us, usually his MO is to connect with us through the kindness of other people — the kind of kindness and love that brings healing, wholeness, and beauty to our lives. You will often find God through the behavior of other people who show you love, care and mercy. to you. God is found whenever and wherever the impulse to love is acted upon.

Robert Schuller once told the story about a prestigious and wealthy man who died in Tennessee. Some very important people showed up to his funeral, and after the funeral service they took their limousines to the cemetery for the graveside. On their way, they saw throngs of people walking down the street to the cemetery. There were so many people that some of them had to walk on the street because the sidewalks were too packed. They were simple people, not well-dressed. There was a man in one of the limousines who wondered to himself, "Are all these people coming to pay their respects to my friend?" He couldn't believe it. When the limousines finally got to the front of the cemetery, it was blocked by all these people, and a police escort had to come in so they could get through. Finally, the curiosity of the man in limousine got the best of him, and he rolled down his window, looked at one of the officers and asked, "Are all these people coming to see my friend?" And the officer sort of said, "No, no, they're here for that funeral of that woman." He said, "A woman? What are you talking about? What person would be so well- known and popular? Who is this woman?" And the officer said, "Well, on your way here, did you pass that school?" The man said, "Yeah." "Well, for thirty years she was the crossing guard there and all these people are the family of all the children she cared for all those years."

God can be found whenever and wherever the impulse to love is acted upon. Now, this is also true when we love other people, we can find God. So if you're in a hurry to find God and you don't want to wait for another person or another experience of receiving love, then just go out and do something lovely for another person. I tell you the truth, you will find God if you do that. If you go out today and act upon that impulse to love, you will find God. Mother Teresa based her whole ministry on this very truth. And when she was asked why she went to Calcutta to care for the sick and the dying in the streets, you know what she said? She said, "In every person I serve, I see the face of Jesus Christ." She based her whole ministry on Jesus' words, "Even if you've done it under the least of these, I tell you you've done it unto me." God is found whenever and wherever the impulse to love is acted upon. You always find God there. So do you have an impulse to love? That's God. What lovely thing can you do for someone in your life right now? You have an instrument, a very powerful instrument, that you probably use just about every day that you can use to do something lovely for another person. I'm talking about a pen.

How many of you keep letters from people that have been written to you over the years? I have a box of letters and cards at home. Whenever I'm discouraged, I just go through these letters and read them, and they always encourage me.

Why not write a letter of encouragement, of kindness, to another person? You never know the difference it's going to make. In fact, right now in the age of email and texts, written letters are special because you hardly ever get them, and they're so deliberate. You never know what a difference it can make to someone who receives an honest, authentic written letter from you that expresses love and kindness. Maya Angelou said, "People will forget what you said, people will forget what you did, but they'll never forget how you made them feel." God is found whenever and wherever the impulse to love is acted upon.

About a half a dozen years ago, there was a story that appeared on CBS News, and it was reported by Steve Hartman. Some of you may know that name, he does a great job reporting on human interest stories. But on this particular story, in this particular story, he talked about a young man by the name of Mitchell Marcus, who was a senior at the time of Coronado High School in El Paso, Texas. You see, Mitchell loved basketball. He always did, from the time he was little. He loved basketball, but Mitchell was developmentally disabled, and he couldn't play for the varsity team. But he was the team's manager and everybody loved him; everybody loved being around him. His enthusiasm for basketball was infectious. Just before the last game of the season, the coach was determined to put Mitchell into the game. Before the game, he said, "Mitchell, I want you to suit up." The coach had decided that whether they were winning or losing, he was going to put Mitchell into the game. In fact, he said even if they lost because of it, he was going to put Mitchell into the game.

The last minute and a half of the game came and the coach put Mitchell into the game. He was so excited. The team did their best to get the ball in his hands so he could score, but it just didn't work. He would shoot the ball and miss, or he would boot the ball out of bounds, giving the ball to the opposing team. But then what happened next was unbelievable. An opponent on the other team got the ball next and said, "Hey, Mitchell," and threw Mitchell the ball. Mitchell took the ball, threw it into the air, and it landed right into the basket.

Now, it wasn't the winning basket, but it didn't matter. The people ran onto the court and they picked Mitchell up. And when the opponent who gave Mitchell the ball was asked why he did it, you know what he said? "I was taught to treat other people the way I want to be treated."

God was in that gym that day, make no mistake about it. For that team love was more important than winning and competition. God is found whenever and wherever the impulse to love is acted upon.

Amen.

Liturgy of the Palms
Luke 19:28-40

The Problem With Palms

Next week churches will have big crowds for Easter. Churches always do. The "Chreasters" come out in droves. The Church alumni will be back for homecoming!

Kidding aside, it is a wonderful sight. It is nice to see churches filled to capacity.

Churches are always looking for ways to draw a big crowd. Recently a church in Maryland came up with a free car giveaway on a Sunday morning. The church bought five cars to give away at worship services.

Pastor Stephen Chandler of Destiny Church in Columbia, Maryland, said his congregation averages about 1,100 on Sundays. When they announced the car giveaway, their attendance more than doubled. The church had so many people attending they added an extra worship service, and another car to give away.

I must admit that doing such stunts to draw a crowd is enticing. The problem is that in order to keep crowds coming back you have to keep doing bigger and better stunts each week. This turns church into a circus and the gospel into a spectacle. It cheapens the ministry of the church. More than that, once the gimmicks are gone and the novelty fades, so do the crowds. When you stop giving people what they want, they will find someone else who will. The sad truth is many people who will be here on Easter won't return until Christmas. It's just the way it is. Crowds are fickle.

Jesus understands this truth better than anyone. If anyone could draw a crowd, it was Jesus. When he emerged on the public scene, he was an overnight sensation. He could not even find a place to be alone. When he came into town, the masses lined the streets. He had a gift for preaching. He mesmerized crowds. He also had the gift of healing. Word spread everywhere that this man from Nazareth healed the sick and raised the dead.

But the big crowds did not adore Jesus for long. The tide began to turn against Jesus. The crowds got smaller and his critics got louder.

44

Earlier Jesus' critics had been afraid to speak out for fear of the masses, but they began to figure out that the fickle public was turning on him. Soon the opposition began to snowball.

The beginning of the end began when Jesus made his triumphal entry, which was shortly before his execution. He entered Jerusalem on a donkey with a big crowd shouting "Hosanna!" But soon the cheering stopped and the crowds faded. And many who were waving palm branches for Jesus were nowhere to be found when he got the tar beat out of him. The shouts of hosanna would give way to "Crucify him!"

Why did the masses so radically turn against Jesus? Why did the cheering stop and the crowds fade? What did he do or say that caused so many to turn their back on him?

In his sermon, "When the Cheering Stopped," my colleague and friend Brett Blair reminded us that one reason why the cheering stopped and the crowds faded was that Jesus began to talk about commitment.

Just before Jesus' triumphal entry, a rich young ruler ran up to Jesus, excited about asking him a question. He said, "What must I do to inherit eternal life?" In other words, "How do I get into heaven?" Jesus replied:

> "Go, sell your possessions and give to the poor, and you will have treasure in heaven. Then come, follow me."
> When the young man heard this, he went away sad, because he had great wealth. — Matthew 19:21-22

The man was stunned by Jesus' response. And so was the crowd who heard it.

I know in my heart when that rich young ruler walked away sorrowfully that day, he was not the only one. I believe many uncommitted people also walked away. Jesus was no longer talking only about grace. He was also talking about the only proper response to God's grace: commitment. And guess what? The masses didn't like it. The masses of today still don't like the idea of commitment.

This is the problem with palms. Palms are beautiful, and we love to see them waved at Jesus. But when palms are cut from trees, they do not live very long. Soon they begin to wither and fade. It is the same with admirers of Jesus. Their enthusiasm may have lasted for a time, but it soon began to fade.

Joseph Bella, a sociologist, wrote a book titled *Habits of the Heart*. In the book he analyzes America, and he says that the symbolic city of America is not New York or Washington, but Las Vegas.

He wrote about a survey he did where he asked Americans what they believed. The most consistent result was that they did not want to commit themselves. He wrote about doing a survey with a girl named Sheila. She said, "I don't want to commit. I just want to feel good all the time about where I am and what I am doing."

Bella said America was covered in Sheilas. Today, our culture is known for its Sheilaism. No one wants to commit to anything. Then folks wonder why they never change, why they never experience life the way they want to. Folks wonder why they have no joy. Joy can only be found by committing to the love of Christ and the purpose Christ has for your life.

Unfortunately, this aversion to commitment has also infected the church. One of the biggest issues confronting the church today is not immorality, sin, worship wars, ethical issues, polity, or corruption. The biggest issue confronting the church today is the growing lack of commitment among the followers of Jesus Christ! We have plenty of admirers of Jesus — those who will tip their hat to Jesus from time to time — those who call themselves fans and throw a dollar in the plate twice a year. But Jesus does not want fans. Jesus wants followers. Jesus does not want admirers. He wants disciples.

For many Christians, commitment to Christ and the church is seen as somewhat of a hobby, an option when the mood is right. "If we don't have weekend plans we will do God a favor and make it to worship... If the kids don't have soccer or we don't get a better offer we will sign up to serve some ministry as long as it fits our schedule... And if we have some money left over after our trips and toys, we may give some of it to the church.

"Oh, and pastor I know I haven't been active in the church for awhile and I gave up that Bible study because I lost interest, but I don't feel very close to God right now... I have thirty minutes. Can you fix me in thirty minutes?"

I agree with the late George Buttrick who said, "Sheep are usually not stolen from the flock, they just nibble themselves away."

Too many Christians base their commitment to Christ and the church on whether or not they "feel like it." Can you imagine what would happen if the rest of the world operated that way? Imagine the fireman saying, "I just don't feel like putting out fires today." Imagine the surgeon saying, "I just don't feel like performing surgery today." Imagine the tired mother awakened in the middle of the night by a crying baby saying, "I just don't feel like feeding the baby." The world would come to a screeching halt!

Yet, when it comes to serving the King of kings, many folks do it only when they feel like it.

So how are you doing? What is your level of commitment? Those of you who joined the church took a vow. You said you would support your church with your prayers, presence, gifts, service and witness. How are you doing with that? Christ died for us and set us free! Do we really have to ponder whether or not we should be faithful? Do we really have to give a second thought to whether or not we should abide in him and grow in our faith?

In order for grace to mean anything there must be a commitment in response to it. Otherwise it is just cheap grace.

Thich leads me to another reason the cheering for Jesus stopped and the crowds faded. Secondly, Blair reminds us that the cheering stopped when Jesus proclaimed that all people are worthy of God's love.

According to Matthew and Luke, right after Jesus' big parade, he went entered the temple to do a little spring cleaning on the money changers. Take a look:

> *Jesus went into the temple courtyard and threw out everyone who was buying and selling there. He overturned the moneychangers' tables and the chairs of those who sold pigeons. He told them, "Scripture says, 'My house will be called a house of prayer,' but you're turning it into a gathering place for thieves!"*
> *Blind and lame people came to him in the temple courtyard, and he healed them. -Matthew 21:12-14*

Notice that after Jesus cleansed the temple he then invites in the lame, the poor, the sick, the outcasts of society and heals them. He brings into God's house what some would call "riff raff."

Jesus was not trying to win friends and influence people. By bringing in these people he was saying all people are loved by God and have access to God. He was showing us what the kingdom of God is going to be like.

Well, the crowds who followed Jesus did not like that then. And they still don't like it today.

Recently, I had a conversation with a friend of mine who shared about the time he was so disgusted with a church that he left it. The pastor felt called to lead the church to participate in a homeless ministry. People were so upset that they fired the pastor!

John 3:16 does not say, "For God so loved the beautiful people" or "the Christians" or "the Republicans" or "Democrats" or "the United Methodists." It says "For God so loved the world."

Christians forget that Jesus said the world will know we are his disciples not by how we worship, not by how we read the bible, not by how we pray, not by the denomination we belong to, but by our love for one another.

I believe another big problem facing the church today is the disparity people experience with Christians who preach love and then act hateful and judgmental. 1 John is clear that it is impossible to love God and hate another person. If we hate another person we need to examine whether we understand the love of God.

Dr. James B. Lemler is an Episcopal priest and he loves to talk about what a second-grade girl said to her parents about his preaching after church one day during Sunday lunch.

In the midst of their conversation, their second-grade daughter sitting at the table chimed in. "Oh, Father Lemler's sermons, they're always the same," she said, "You know… blah, blah, blah, … love … blah, blah, blah … love." Dr. Lemler said he was amused and thought to himself, "Hey, this little girl really got it. Over and over again…blah, blah, blah, love… blah, blah, blah, love…." "Blah, blah, blah love…" (http://day1.org/1094-blah_blah_blah_blah_love).

I hope when I am eulogized that is exactly what people say about my preaching — "…blah, blah, blah, love."

But would you believe there are some who have a problem with loving all people. That's why the cheering stopped for Jesus. He opened the doors of the church to everyone. It angered some people then and it still angers some people today.

But that love would soon be demonstrated in a way that would transform the world. And that leads me to that last reason the cheering stopped and the crowds faded. Blair reminds us that Jesus began to talk about a cross. Take a look:

From that time on Jesus began to explain to his disciples that he must go to Jerusalem and suffer many things...and that he must be killed and on the third day be raised to life.

Peter took him aside and began to rebuke him. "Never, Lord!" he said. "This shall never happen to you!"

Jesus turned and said to Peter, "Get behind me, Satan! You are a stumbling block to me; you do not have in mind the concerns of God, but merely human concerns." — Matthew 16:21-23

Some wanted Jesus to be a revolutionary. Some wanted him to be a great political figure to further their agenda but his whole purpose since the beginning was to show this world that the only thing that can defeat hate, death, sin, evil, and darkness is God's sacrificial and reconciling love.

A few years ago, Mark Trotter told a true story about a man in New York City who was kidnapped. His kidnappers called his wife and asked for $100,000 ransom. She talked them down to $30,000. The story had a happy ending: the man returned home unharmed, the money was recovered, and the kidnappers were caught and sent to jail.

Commenting on this incident, Calvin Trillin wrote, "Don't you know the man's conversation with his wife was very interesting when he found out his wife got him back for a discount?" Calvin Trillin wrote about this incident. He imagined out loud what the negotiations must have been like: "$100,000 for that old guy? You have got to be crazy. Just look at him! Look at that gut! You want $100,000 for that? You've got to be kidding. Give me a break here. $30,000 is my top offer."

Mark Trotter concluded his rendition of the story with this thoughtful comment:

> *I am not sure who you relate to in that story, but I relate to the husband. I'd like to think if I were in a similar situation, there would be people who would spare no expense to get me back. They wouldn't haggle over the price. They wouldn't say, 'Well, let me think about it.' I like to think that they would say, 'We'll do anything for you'* ("It's Ok to be Extravagant" by James Moore).

Guess what? Christ did. He did everything for you.

> *"You have been bought and paid for by Christ, so you belong to him — be free now from all these earthly prides and fears." — 1 Corinthians 7:23 TLB*

God says that you're not only accepted, you're also valuable.

You have been bought and paid for by Christ. You belong to Jesus. You are accepted, and you are valuable! What Christ has done for us demands a response — a response of commitment to love as Jesus loved and to serve as Jesus served. Are you an admirer of Jesus or a follower?

Amen.

I am grateful for Brett Blair and his sermon "When the Cheering Stopped." It was a valuable resource for me as I prepared this message.

Do You Want The Truth?

Have you ever tried to guess where people are from by the way they talk? The other day I was chatting with a nurse about her husband who plays golf. She said, "He's wicked good." I said, "Massachusetts or Maine?" She said, "I'm from Maine. How did you know?" I said, "Nobody down here says wicked unless it's Halloween."

I remember when my step sisters and brothers would come visit us from Chicago, we would get the biggest kick out of their thick accents. And they would get the biggest kick out of ours! They always laughed when we said, "Y'all." We would say, "Well, when you are talking to a group, what do you say, "You all"? "No, we say, "Hey, You Guys!"

And then we would go out to eat with them and they would ask the waiter, "What kind of pop do you have?" Pop? What's pop? You know soda pop." Oh, you mean Coke. That's always a dead give away that someone is from Atlanta. They refer to all brands of soda as "Coke" even if it's not Coke. And Atlantans never say "Co-ca Co-la", nor "At-lan-ta". You drink a "Cocola in Atlanna." Am I right? (based on a Facebook post, source unknown)

Yeah, sometimes it's easy to tell where people are from by the way they talk.

And sometimes you can even guess who people are and maybe what they do by the way they dress and carry themselves.

One time I was in a bank and I was chatting with the teller. She said, "You're a preacher, ain't ya?" "How did you know?" "I don't know. You just seem like a preacher. The way you talk and handle yourself." Well, I wasn't wearing a clergy collar and I certainly wasn't pronouncing a blessing on the bank that day. Perhaps it was just my holy glow?

Of course, sometimes people can fool you. They can put on a real good act. They are not who they claim to be. I had a friend who was a real practical joker. One night we were eating at a Rio Bravo Mexican restaurant. He bought one of their hats and began walking around the restaurant acting like the manager. And people believed him! He carried himself with confidence. Just began walking around tables asking people how their meals were. It was hysterical. Before we left, he did a rather cruel thing. He approached a big table of people and asked them how their meal was. Then he said, "Tell you what, have a dessert on us tonight!" And then we left. Can you imagine?

He had them fooled. He looked like a manager. Talked like manager. But he wasn't a real manager.

I remembered being fooled by a lady who came to a previous church needing money. She didn't look destitute. She was well groomed and well spoken. She told me she went to my Alma Mater Florida Southern. Talked about places in and around the school. Then she shared a very believable story about her needing money to pay for rent. We wrote a check to the apartment complex, thinking it was legit. Later, we came to find out that she was in cahoots with the apartment manager and they were stealing money from churches. She had made everything up and was very convincing. And believe me, I don't get fooled easily. But I was that day.

Sometimes it is easy to tell who people are. And sometimes it's not.

I wonder if it's easy for people to tell that we are Christians. I wonder how people can really tell that we are true blue followers of Jesus Christ. No pretending. Do we have a dead give-away? What do you think might convince them to say, "Yep. Yep, they are a Christian"? Is it by the way we talk or the way we don't talk? Is it the way we dress or the way we carry ourselves? Is it our habits? Our kindness to others? Or is it simply because we claim to be Christians and our names are on a church roll?

I remember hearing a fiery preacher at a conference as a teenager. He got all lathered up and said, "If you were put on trial for being a Christian, would there be enough evidence to convict you?"

I am sure some of you have heard that one before. It's not a bad question, you know. The witness says, "Yeah, he's my neighbor. I once saw a Bible in his car. And every Sunday morning I see he and his family dressed real nice going to church. They must be Christians. I will testify that they are Christians."

Another witness says, "Well, no I watched the same family fighting in the parking lot of the church. Screaming and yelling...not so sure...."

The lawyer says, "Well, what about this person? Do you think they are a Christian?

Witness says, "Well, I have never heard him say a cuss word. He never loses his temper. And in traffic I have seen him let people in ahead of him....Oh, one time I heard him praying on the golf course. At least...I think that is what he was doing? Yeah, I will testify that he is a Christian."

Is that enough evidence you think? Would that really convince someone?

I remember giving a kid a ride to school one time. We were in high school. Parents very strict. Went to church whenever the doors opened. Wouldn't let the kid do anything fun. Wasn't allowed to go to prom. Wasn't allowed to listen to secular music. He looked down on my floor and he saw a CD. It was Def Leppard's "Hysteria". He was shocked. You would've thought it had been a book on witchcraft. He said, "Do your parents know you have this? Do you not believe in God or something?"

I got a phone call many years ago when I was serving my very first church. I was really wet behind the ears. It was a small country church and one of my members was calling me all upset. "I need to talk to you." He came over and sat down in my little office and said, "People are talking. And folks are really disappointed in you. We may have to talk to SPR about this."

"What is it?" "Well, there is a rumor going around that you were at a bar the other night. Please tell me this is not true." "Well, yes it's true. The place is called Applebee's and it was very crowded. The only table we could find was in the bar."

Oh, it was a real scandal for a while. But I got away with it.

Some people think the strongest evidence that we are Christians is found in our ability to follow rules, following the do's and dont's. Not misbehaving. Not drinking or smoking or cussing. Good church attendance. Being good boys and girls.

But the good Protestants among us strongly disagree, don't we? "No, no Charley, the strongest evidence is faith. Did they repent of their sin and give their lives to Jesus Christ? Remember Ephesians said, "We are saved by grace through faith, not by our works, lest any man should boast.""

The defendant said, "Yes, I am saved. I am a Christian. When I was a teenager, I came down the aisle and accepted Christ and was baptized. I am a Christian! I can show you the place in my Bible where my pastor signed his name next to the date of my baptism."

"Did anyone witness this?"

The witness said, "Yes, yes, I remember. He is telling the truth. I was there. I saw him do it. He looked like a drowned rat coming out of that water. There were tears coming down his face. It looked real to me. I even saw him on the street one day sharing the five spiritual laws to a complete stranger. I heard him ask the man, 'If you died tonight, do you know where you would spend eternity?' Yeah, that's enough evidence to convince me. I'd say he was a Christian."

Do you think that's the strongest evidence? Would that be enough to convince people?

No, no Charley, remember Jesus said, "The world will know you are my disciples if you have love for one another." And the book of James plainly says, "Faith without works is dead." That's much stronger evidence. That's the real stuff. Are people walking their talk? Are they backing up all their preaching about love with action? Those folks are the true Christians. That's how you can tell.

A witness says, "Yeah, I believe she is a Christian. I have seen her help out in the soup kitchen. I've heard she visits people in the hospital. She takes the altar flowers to the nursing homes every week. She tutors underprivileged kids at the local school. Only a Christian would do that. She must follow Jesus."

Well, it's hard to argue with that. Many people believe our kindness toward others is the strongest evidence that what we are Christians.

I wonder where Jesus would land on all of this? I guess he's the one who really counts, right? Does Jesus believe us? Is he convinced? What do you think convinces Jesus that we are serious about following him? You know, throughout his ministry Jesus was highly suspicious of people who wanted to follow him. He knew he had admirers. Fans. And he had some hard things to say to them:

> "No one who puts a hand to the plow and looks back is fit for service in the kingdom of God." – Luke 9:62

> "If any want to become my followers, let them deny themselves and take up their cross and follow me." – Matthew 16:24

And whoever does not carry their cross and follow me cannot be my disciple. – Luke 14:27

Those of you who do not give up everything you have cannot be my disciples. – Luke 14:33

Wait, Wait, back up Charley. Now, that's another matter altogether. Who can do that? Isn't following the rules enough? Isn't having faith in Jesus enough? Isn't being kind to others enough? I mean, I thought we had all of this Christian faith business figured out. Put your faith in Jesus. Behave. Be kind to people. Go to church. Isn't that what it's all about?

Apparently there is something else Jesus is looking for in those who would be his followers.

In our text for today Jesus is before Pilate. The religious community wants him executed and they want Pilate to do their dirty work.

Jesus knows whatever he says to Pilate could get him killed. Later, in John's version of the event Jesus says something to Pilate that defines his ministry. Defines who he is. "You can call me king or whatever you like, but I will tell you why I was born: to testify to the truth of God, that God is real. You can take me now and torture me but my purpose is to bear witness to the truth of God at all costs."

That's our Jesus! Isn't it? Going all the way for us. No compromising. He resisted the devil in the wilderness, he defied the rich and powerful. Telling like it is….

Then Jesus said something else. Are you listening? "My followers, those who belong to the truth, those who take root in me, those who draw life from me, will listen to my voice and do what I do. In a moment of truth, they will not compromise. They will be obedient as I have been obedient."

Could it be that a real follower of Jesus is one who, well, looks like Jesus? Could it be when faced with a moment of truth a follower of Jesus will listen to the voice of Jesus and be obedient, even if it costs them?

Yeah, yeah, I get it Charley. I have heard those stories. They put a gun to a man's head and they say if you don't renounce your faith, we are going to kill you. Or Rosa Parks resisting the authorities and remaining seated in the white section of the bus. Or those whistle blowers who bring down an entire corporation because of their greed. We admire people like that. They are heroes.

But, most of us live very ordinary lives. We don't face such moments of truth. Oh, I don't know about that.

You're at a party with all of your friends. Everyone is having fun and telling jokes. And then someone starts to tell racist jokes…What do you do? Listen to Jesus and walk away or laugh with them to be part of the group?

You're in the lunch room at school and you see the bullied kid sitting by himself eating his lunch. Your friends are saving your seat like they always do and they are calling you over. What do you do? Do you listen to voice of Jesus telling you to sit with him and risk getting ridiculed yourself?

Your estranged brother calls you. You have been bitter about him for years. You say you will never forgive him for what he did. You don't answer and send it to voice mail. He wants to reconcile. Do you listen to the voice of Jesus or do you ignore it?

"Fred Craddock once decided to go back home for a visit when he was on school break. It is no place special on the map. It is just a little town in Arkansas. On the first morning of his visit he ventured downtown. He walked into the diner that had been there for a hundred years. Fred just wanted to sit there, eat breakfast and remember simpler times. He said the place had not changed. Everything was identical to his youth, even the owner.

"As Fred waited for his fried eggs, the owner walked up to him and said, "I know you! You used to live here. You went on to be a preacher! I need to talk to you." Fred nodded yes, but he thought, "Just go away! All I want is breakfast and some quiet."

"The owner pulled up a chair and began to talk. He said to Fred, "I don't know what to do." Fred said, "About what?" The owner responded, "About the curtain!" He motioned to the curtain and Fred looked. The curtain had been there for years. Fred remembered that curtain from his childhood. The curtain wasn't there just for decorative purposes. It had a practical purpose. The curtain was there to separate the white customers from the black customers. The white customers would enter the restaurant through the front door and ate on that side of the curtain. The black customers entered through the back door and ate on that side of the curtain.

"Just then, Fred's breakfast was delivered. He wanted the owner to finish up his story because his eggs were getting cold. To hasten it along, Fred asked the owner, 'What is the problem?' (Fred knew the problem.) The owner said, 'Should I take the curtain down or should I leave the curtain up?' Fred gave him a blank look and the owner continued. 'If I take the curtain down, I will lose my business. If I leave the curtain up, I will lose my soul!' " (taken from a transcript from an unknown source).

When it counts, do we listen to the voice of Jesus or do we ignore it? Oh, listening to Jesus, being a follower, will cost you, no doubt about it. But at the end of the day as you are getting into bed thinking about what you did and the consequences of it, if you listen closely, you will hear Jesus say to you, "I saw what you did today. I have been telling the angels about it. I couldn't be prouder of you."

Amen.

How Not To Grow A Church

In one of her sermons, the great preacher Barbara Brown Taylor boldly declared that Jesus would have been a terrible pastor. I believe she is right. The teachings of Jesus aren't exactly Ted Talks on how to attract a crowd for Sunday worship.

Imagine an SPR committee interviewing a potential pastor the bishop would like to appoint to their church:

"Yes, very nice to meet you, Reverend. Tell us, what is your understanding of being a Christian?"

"The first rule is you must hate your father and mother, your wife and children, your brothers and sisters--yes, even your own life. Jesus said that anyone who is not prepared to give up everything cannot be a member."

"Um, well thank you. We will be in touch. Don't call us. We'll call you."

After being a pastor for several years, I have learned that if you want to grow a church, you have to create an attractive environment that meets the needs of people. Or, to put it bluntly, you must give people what they want so they don't go to a church down the road.

And once you get people here, you have to keep them here. So, worship and preaching need to be inspiring and meaningful. Opportunities for Christian education should be offered for all ages and must be stimulating, varied and convenient. And there should be ample opportunities for service and fellowship. That's the way you grow a church.

When I was serving another church, a lady I had never met came to see me in my office one day. Apparently, she had just left another church in frustration and was looking for a new one. I asked her why she had left the church. She said, "I wasn't being fed. And my needs weren't being met." She continued, "I have checked your services online and you don't seem like a bad preacher and your church seems to be doing a lot of good things. I think I will give your church a try. But, before I do, I have some expectations."

She then pulled out a piece of paper with a long list of things she expected, including the proper length of sermons, types of hymns to be sung, particular Sunday school curriculum, and more.

When I thought she was finished, I asked, "Anything else?" She replied, "Yes, and the sanctuary should not be too cold." I almost gave her the line from Burger King, "Your way, right away!" but I didn't. I would find out later from some other pastors in the community that this particular person was a "frequent shopper" of churches.

There is nothing wrong with expecting a church to meet your needs. The only problem is that Jesus said that if we want to follow him, our needs will not be a priority. In fact, they are virtually irrelevant. Jesus said that unless we are willing to hate our families, carry our crosses, and give up everything that is dear to us, we can't be his disciples. In our text for today in John, Jesus piles on and says that we also have to wash feet and love everyone.

I must say that Jesus is not really much help in the church growth department. We like to say that the Bible has many answers to the questions of life and ministry, but building a booming church that meets everyone's needs is not one of them.

If I took Jesus' words as seriously as I should, I would have ushers and greeters greeting new people at the door, not with a bulletin, but with a clipboard with a list of questions:

"Are you absolutely sure you want to follow this way of life?"

"Are you absolutely sure you are willing to give Jesus everything you have?"

"Are you absolutely sure you are willing to put aside everything that matters to you for the sake of the gospel, even family?"

"If you are not, you may want to go home and think this over. This is not a country club you're joining."

I think it is safe to say that this approach is not the way to grow a church.

Barbara Brown Taylor said, "If Jesus were in charge of an average congregation there would be about four people left there on Sunday morning, and chances are those four would be fooling themselves."

One of the things that Jesus said that bothers most of us are these words "Hate father and mother, wife and children, brothers and sisters, yes, an even life itself…" Hate? Jesus is teaching us to hate? Doesn't that cancel out everything Jesus taught us about loving one another?

Take some comfort from the fact that Jesus was using an old Semitic expression that means to "detach oneself from, to turn away from." It was a figure of speech we don't use anymore. Barbara Brown Taylor reminds us that "In Jesus' day you expressed your preference for something by pairing two things and saying you loved one but disliked the other." In other words, "I love the Georgia Bulldogs but hate the Georgia Tech Yellow Jackets." Jesus' use of the word hate didn't have anything to do with hating something in the way we experience it. It was about priorities.

But, if we are honest, there is little consolation in that explanation because Jesus is plainly laying out what is costs to follow him and it's no picnic. Jesus does divide families and loyalties. He does create chaos and turn lives upside down.

I remember a classmate of mine in seminary. He was middle aged, second career. He had a good life and a good career, and then God called him to preach. How inconvenient. His wife and family lived in another state, so he would go to class during the week and travel back to his family on the weekends. I recall him coming into class one day looking very upset. When I asked him what was wrong, he said, "I spoke with my wife last night. She said I have to make a choice." She said, "It's me or the ministry. I don't want to be married to a preacher." The next semester he was in one of my classes. I guess he made his choice. I guess he took Jesus seriously.

Much of what Jesus said is hard to swallow, but honestly, I think Jesus is really doing us a favor. He is telling us what we are getting ourselves into. Jesus was headed to Jerusalem, and he knew what awaited him. He also knew what awaited those who claimed to follow him. It wasn't going to be pretty. He did not want them and doesn't want us to have any illusions about what it means to be his disciples.

You don't follow a man like Jesus without running into problems. Jesus wasn't killed for saying, "I am here to make life easier and more peaceful for you." Will Willimon reminds us that Jesus was killed for saying, "The poor are precious and the religious and privileged are in trouble; Not everyone who cries, 'Lord, Lord' will get into God's kingdom. In fact, prostitutes, tax collectors, and vile sinners will get in before you!"

You don't say things like that without getting into deep trouble. And you certainly don't follow a guy like that without creating problems for yourself. Willimon asserts that the problem with Jesus is not that we find him unclear or confusing. It is that we find him too darn difficult and demanding. This Jesus is relentless, and here we are to-day wanting to follow him?

I remember a man coming up to me after a service and saying, "I didn't like your sermon today. In fact, I don't like a lot of your sermons."

"Oh really? Well, thanks for your honesty. Why is that? Do tell."

"Well, your sermons make me feel uncomfortable. I don't come to church for that. I come to church for some peace and comfort."

I said, "Well, you picked the wrong faith. I didn't have problems until I met Jesus."

Then he said, "And that's another thing, if I was a preacher, I wouldn't spend so much time on those difficult sayings of Jesus. They are too hard. People aren't going to do those things. You're wasting your time."

Maybe he was right. Maybe I am wasting my time preaching on Jesus. I have to say I have struggled a great deal to find a digestible lesson for you today. In my preaching classes, I teach my students that if you want your sermon to be sharp, clear and powerful you must prepare it around one clear, compelling point. Well, it has been challenging to come up with that point. This preaching thing is not as easy as it looks!

All week long I have thought about what the point my sermon should be. First, I thought, maybe I should tell them following Jesus is not for everyone. There is a difference between being saved and being a disciple. If you don't think you have what it takes, that's ok. Just try to be a good person from time to time and come to church every once in a while.

Then I thought, no that's too soft. I should tell them that Jesus is calling us to get our lives together and priorities straight. Jesus and the church should be our number one priority, above all else. No more spiritual apathy! Get busy loving people, even if they are unlovable and washing feet, even if they are dirty. That wouldn't be a bad ser-mon. I have actually preached those sermons.

But the more I thought and prayed about some of the hard things that Jesus said the more it became clear to me that I must warn all of us about Jesus.

A colleague of mine had a good friend he went to college with. They remained good friends after they graduated. My colleague's friend became very successful and wealthy at a young age. He had three or four homes. He was a member of a half dozen prestigious golf clubs. He had all the nice cars and toys with all the bells and whistles. He would joke with my colleague about not having kids: "You can't have kids and keep a scratch handicap." Besides, he and his wife loved to travel and didn't want to be tied down.

One day, my colleague could not find or contact his friend. He looked everywhere — social media, contacted other friends. It seemed like his friend dropped off the face of the earth. My colleague thought maybe he and his wife were on a long trip to Europe.

Well, there came a time when my colleague took a group of adults on a mission trip and they visited an orphanage they had heard about. It was run by a couple that adopted several kids and had taken in many more. They had a staff of people helping. When my colleague walked into that house, he almost fell on the floor. There was his friend changing a diaper in a t-shirt and shorts. He and his wife had given up their lavish lifestyle to run an orphanage.

My colleague was dying to find out what had caused his friend's dramatic transformation. So, later that night, after they had put all the kids to bed, they sat in the small living room and talked. "What happened to you?" my colleague asked. "Well, you are not going to believe this, but I was on a business trip and a co-worker of mine kept bugging me to go on this spiritual retreat. So, finally, I went begrudgingly. One night, I heard a man speak about his ministry to orphans and something happened to me. It was like an out of body experience. Something grabbed my heart and wouldn't let go. Afterward, I called my wife and told her that things were about to change." Then he said, "If I had known how much Jesus was going to change my life I would have never gone near a retreat or a church. I was just minding my own business and out of nowhere Jesus grabbed my heart. There is no going back now."

It is dangerous to follow Jesus because Jesus changes you. Suddenly, you see the world through the eyes of Jesus and it changes your heart. You see all the pain and hurt and want to heal it. You see all the dirty feet and you want to wash them. You see all that needs to change and you want to change it. And you are willing to do anything and everything and give up anything and everything to get it done.

Are we ready for that kind of change?

Fair warning. We are playing with fire. Jesus is not interested in growing churches: he wants to grow disciples. So, this Jesus we pray to, sing to, preach, and teach about, is not messing around. He is on the move and his love is relentless, even reckless. I would watch your heart because he just might change you so much that everything you think is important won't mean that much to you anymore. All you will care about is being the hands and feet of Christ. If you are not prepared for that kind of transformation, don't follow Jesus.

You've been warned. Jesus has warned all of us.

Amen.

Barbara Brown Taylor's message "High Priced Discipleship" and Will Willimon's sermon, "Who Do You Say that I Am" were helpful resources for me as I prepared this sermon.

Good Friday
John 18:1-19, 42

Dying To Live

They say you can't talk about three things: Religion, sex, and politics. Well, I think "they" are wrong, whoever "they" are. We do talk about those things. We're just terrible at it.

However, there is one subject most of us avoid like the plague: death. Yes, we are sad when a loved one dies and we will attend the funeral and acknowledge death. But we don't really talk about death and the deeper meaning of it. Truthfully, we either deny it or avoid it. No one wants to think about death.

Of course, the kicker is that dying is exactly what Jesus Christ calls his followers to do. If you really want to experience what it means to be a Christian, if you really want to experience the joy of following Christ, if you really want to find life, hope, and resurrection in your life, Jesus said, you must first die. You have to die in order to live.

Now if that seems counterintuitive, you're right. It is. In fact, much of what Jesus had to say was counterintuitive and filled with paradox. Jesus said, "It is only in giving that you receive." He also said, "If you want to be first, you must become last" and "If you're going to be master, you must first become a servant." Jesus also said, "If you want to find your life, you're going to have to lose it."

And all of these ironic statements can be summed up in one sentence: *We must die if we want to live.*

Jesus says more about this in John:

> *Very truly I tell you, unless a kernel of wheat falls to the ground and dies, it remains only a single seed. But if it dies, it produces many seeds. Anyone who loves their life will lose it, while anyone who hates their life in this world will keep it for eternal life. -John 12:24-25*

Throughout his ministry Jesus was constantly teaching us that death must precede birth. There is no resurrection without a crucifixion. A seed must be buried before it can grow.

I am not talking about physical death, although we as Christian believe that our physical death will lead to life everlasting, just as Jesus promised and demonstrated. I am talking about dying on an emotional level, spiritual level, even a material level. I am talking about dying to self and being prepared to surrender to God those things we think we can't live without. We think we can't live without certain things. Christ tells us we can't truly live if we hold on to those things.

Now, that's not what you, me, or anyone wants to hear. We don't want to have to give up anything in order to gain something. We resist death and loss with great stubbornness.

In our assigned passage from John 18, we notice Simon Peter finding it very difficult to die to self and yield to Christ. He couldn't hold back his sword and he didn't have the courage to confess that he was a follower of Christ. His safety and the warmth of a fire on a cold night were hard to resist. It is difficult to die.

Barbara Brown Taylor remembered the time she witnessed a protest to death. She was attending an Easter Vigil at Christ Church in New Haven, Connecticut, and the time came for a three-year-old named Ellen to be baptized. Nothing unusual about it except that the three-year-old's parents wanted her to be baptized by immersion. This is a problem with a church which only has a bird-bath sized baptismal font.

Still, the priest agreed and came up with a 36-gallon garbage can decorated with ivy. It was not pretty, but it suited the purpose. When the priest bent down to pick Ellen up, she screamed, "Don't do it!" She planted her feet against the garbage can, causing the water to spill on the floor. Again, she screamed, "Don't do it!"

Taylor does not remember whether or not Ellen did it, but she can still hear that child's protest ringing through the rafters of the church. Though only three years old, Ellen believed she would die and wanted no part of it (Taylor, "Buried by Baptism").

Like Ellen, we really don't any part of it, either! When we feel God leading us to leave sin behind, we shout, "Don't do it!" When we hear God calling us out of our comfort zones, we scream, "Don't do it!" When we feel God pulling us away from our past, we hang on tooth and nail and scream, "Don't do it!" Most of us go kicking and screaming into death. We don't want to lose those things we hold dear.

I wish I could tell you that there is an easier way to grow and find life, but there isn't one. All of us must die in order to give birth to something new. A bad habit must die to provide room for a good one. Certain ways of thinking must change in order to get the desired action. A place of comfort must be left in order to move to a healthier one. All such radical changes must occur in order for something new to be born.

Just listen to newborns scream as they make their miraculous move from the familiar womb into a foreign world. It must be awful for them, but there is no other way for birth to happen.

Ask a recent graduate how difficult it is to leave college and enter a new world of responsibility. Such change is tough but without making that leap there is no opportunity, growth or accomplishment.

Ask a couple how challenging it is to let go of their own pursuits in order to raise a child. A big sacrifice, but there is no greater joy than raising a child.

We must die in order to live. We must be broken in order to be made whole. We must give in order to receive.

J. Wallace Hamilton once called on a home and found the mother of the house in her garden. She was down on her knees in an onion patch plucking out the weeds. She kept working as he talked to her. As they spoke, he noticed she was not only picking out the weeds, she was plucking out good onions, young ones, small throwing them away with the weeds. He said, "Why are you throwing away those perfectly good onions?"

She replied, "You've never gardened, have you? There are too many onions in this bed. I have to pick out some of them to give the rest a chance to grow. To leave them all here would mean they would all grow up to be little spindly things and none of them would be robust and healthy."

Commenting on that conversation Hamilton said, "There are times when the divine gardener must do that. Growing in our hearts are too many desires, conflicting, competing desires. We want too many things . . . so the divine gardener thins them out, cuts them off to give the best a change to grow" ("When Disappointment is a Door" by J. Wallace Hamilton).

The gifted writer Urban T. Holmes III made this clear for us: "Any good gardener knows that beautiful roses require careful pruning. Pieces of living plant have to die. It cannot just grow wild."

The same is true of us. Parts of us need to die if we are to become the person that is in God's vision.

I think of what was needed to die in my life in order to give room for the joy of my son Paul. Before Paul, I used to think about all of the things I was able to do because I did not have kids. Things like golfing, traveling, reading, and setting more ambitious goals. All great things, but many of those aspirations had to die to make room for the joy of Paul. And now I wouldn't trade being a father for any of those things!

I have also learned over the years that certain ways of thinking and attitudes had to die in order for me to be the person and minister God has called me to be. For example, I used to be a victim of the comparison trap. I used to compare myself to other preachers and think that if I did not attain their success or do what they did I was not worthy or successful. As I have matured, I have learned that God calls each of us to our own unique journeys and success is being faithful to that particular journey. God calls me to be me, not someone else. I have had to let comparisons die to be at peace with who God has destined me to be and find true joy in my journey.

What do you need to make room for in order for God's will and joy to enter your life? What needs to die in your life so you can truly live? I can't think of a better time to ask ourselves that question than on Good Friday.

Do you remember what Paul said?

> *"How can we who died to sin go on living in it? Do you not know that all of us who have been baptized into Christ Jesus were baptized into his death?*
> *"We were therefore buried with him through baptism into death in order that, just as Christ was raised from the dead through the glory of the Father, we too may live a new life. For if we have been united with him in a death like his, we will certainly also be united with him in a resurrection like his." – Romans 6:2-5*

Someone once said that these powerful verses teach us that "each death hides a resurrection." There is no need to be afraid of letting certain things die in your life because the promise is that there is a resurrection hidden within each death.

I am reminded of someone I know who battled alcoholism for years. A couple of years ago she was arrested for driving drunk and hit rock bottom. It was a death. She felt the tremendous toll it had on her, her family and on her finances. But a resurrection occurred as she allowed certain unhealthy things to die in her life. Here is a portion of an email she sent me:

"It's weird... I feel like things are just falling into place since I 'broke' and started putting my life in *God's* hands. It's like the beautiful puzzle is just snapping together. Random pieces are just falling into place. Cheesy, but that's how it feels."

I replied, "That's so awesome! It's amazing what happens when we surrender. Jesus said it: 'Those who lose their life will find it.'"

Jesus' very life and death gave us the greatest example of today's message. Can you imagine all that Christ had to give up? Remember he was also human. His ambitions had to die. His desire for a long and prosperous life with a family had to die. His own will had to die. His true moment of death was not his last breath on the cross. His true moment of death came when he prayed, "Not my will but yours be done." But because he was willing to die, he lived! He was resurrected! And his promise to us is that we will live too. Therefore, we don't have to be afraid of death, any death.

This leads me to tell you what it means to be a Christian. If you are confused about all this death business and what it has to do with being a Christian, then listen up. The key to understanding this mystery of dying to live and following Christ is seen one verse tucked in the book of Galatians:

> *I have been crucified with Christ; it is no longer I who live, but Christ lives in me. -Galatians 2:20*

Now take a look at the last four words in this verse: *Christ lives in me.* James Merritt lifts these words up as way of thinking about the word "Christian." He said it is a combination of two words: Christ + In. Or Christian. What does this mean? You cannot live the Christian life on your own. The only way you can live it is by "Christ living in you." So, as James Merritt says, "You can boil Christianity down to one single simple sentence — Jesus gave his life *for* me so he could live his life *in* me." Another way to put it is "the Christian life is not you living for Jesus; it is Jesus living in you!" ("Live and Let Die" by James Merritt).

Merritt remembered getting a letter years ago from a man in his church concerning his four-year-old granddaughter. His son-in-law is a surgeon, and both his grandson and granddaughter were involved in this precious story.

His son-in-law got a call one morning for an emergency surgery. When he got home after the surgery his son asked his dad about it. He said, "Dad, did you have to cut the man open to see what was inside of him?" The dad said, "Yes, son, I did." He said, "Dad, did you see his lungs and his stomach, and could you see his heart?" His dad said, "Yes, son, I could." Well, at that moment his little four-year-old granddaughter who had been intently listening to the conversation, immediately looked up at her dad with big wide eyes of amazement, and said, "Dad, you did see his heart?" The dad said, "Yes, I did." She said, "Dad, did you see Jesus in his heart?" (Merritt).

That's what it truly means to follow Jesus. He comes to live in your heart and the world can see him living in you.

So, what do you need to give up in order to live? What needs to die so you can find life in Christ and Christ in you?

Resurrection of the Lord
John 20:1-18 or Luke 24:1-12

Do You Believe In Easter?

Do you believe in Easter? Perhaps some of you are skeptical. Maybe you enjoy the trappings of this day, but you are still not sure about this resurrection business.

Bishop William Willimon tells of visiting a man with only a couple of days left to live. He asked the man whether he was fearful. To Willimon's surprise the man replied, "Fear? No! I'm not fearful because of my faith in Jesus."

"Yes," said Willimon. "We all have hope that our future is in God's hands."

"Well, I am not hopeful because of what I believe about the future. I am hopeful because of what I have experienced in the past."

The man continued, explaining, "I look back over my life, all the mistakes I've made, all the times I've turned away from Jesus, gone my own way, strayed and gotten lost. And time and time again, he found a way to get to me, looked for me when I wasn't looking for him. I don't think he will let something like my dying defeat his love for me."

Now there's a man who knew how much God loved him. Can you believe God loves you that much? That's one reason some people have difficulty believing in the resurrection. They have a problem believing that God really loves them that much.

Well, I am here to tell you that he does. Easter means God's love is real and stronger than death. Easter means that you will never be separated from God's love. This means believing in Easter, believing in this death defeating love, can change your life.

And this Easter love is not just available after death but is available now. We not only have resurrection power in death, but we also have it in life. It is something that transforms you.

Respected theologian Wolfhart Pannenberg once put it this way, "The evidence for Jesus' resurrection is so strong that nobody would question it except for two things: First, it is a very unusual event. And second, if you believe it happened, you have to change the way you live."

Did you catch that? "If you believe it happened, you have to change the way you live." The power of God's love changes you. It certainly changed the disciples. One day they were too terrified and the next day they were filled with resurrection power and shared the good news to everyone.

The power of God is unmatched! The same power that created you — the same power that raised Jesus from the dead can empower you to rise above anything in life. On this Easter morning I have some great news to share with you.

You Can Rise Above Discouragement

Allow me to ask you a vital question. Are you living the life you were intended to live? Is the real you alive or asleep? Henry Thoreau once said, "Most people are living lives of quiet desperation." Does this describe you today? Oh maybe you have shown up for Easter worship today and you look bright and cheery on the outside, but inside you are desperate to really live.

When God created you, he gave you creativity, genius and joy. What has happened to that person? Well, you have grown up and you have listened to other voices tell you what you should or should not do. The pressures of life and the expectations of others have caused you to become cynical. One day you woke up and realized you were numb and the real person inside you is asleep.

Arthur Caliandro remembered reading an arresting statement by Bernie Segal, the great doctor and writer. Segal said, "I see so many people who have died to stay alive." Segal went on to describe what he meant by the statement by saying, "I see individuals who become people they don't want to be. They have allowed themselves to be forced into roles that are meaningless to them. You know, people can commit suicide without hurting themselves physically." It can happen. Through defeat and compromise we can kill the authentic person inside of us.

The great news on this Easter day is you can decide to be a new creation. You can claim the person God had created you to be!

Susan Sparks reminded us that deep down, the human soul yearns for joy, yearns to soar. Spark compared it to the movie *Mary Poppins*, a movie I watched over and over again as a kid. Without a doubt my favorite scene is the one where Uncle Albert starts laughing in that lifeless, sterile bank vault. As he laughs with joy, he begins to float up to the ceiling. The laughter, life, and passion he felt brought him a lightness that made him float. And everyone around him began to laugh and float up as well.

That scene gets to the root of a deep human truth: We all have a soul that yearns for joy and lightness — a soul that yearns to soar. We all have been made for greatness. We know that deep within us. But the distractions of life so often get in the way. And then we begin to seek the living among the dead, and slowly we can become the living dead — no life, no purpose, no joy, no passion, no vision — all because we forget the truth of this glorious day. All because we forget where real life is found. But the power of the resurrection helps us rise above discouragement.

You Can Rise Above Despair

Our text for today tells us that on that first Easter morning Mary Magdalene went to the tomb "while it was still dark." So often we picture this scene at sunrise with the sun shining brightly on Mary. But the text says it was "early." "Early" meant between 3 and 6am. In other words, when Mary went to the tomb it was very dark.

It was the darkest hour for Mary. Mary was marginalized in life. Jesus came alongside of her and changed her life. He gave her a worth that she never knew she could have. However, they took her Lord away and beat him, mocked him, and crucified him. Mary's dreams were shattered.

Later in the story, Mary was at the tomb in the dark with tears in her eyes. She made out a figure coming toward her and she thought it was the gardener. She couldn't see that it was Jesus. She was desperate and asked, "What have you done with the body of my Lord?" What did Jesus do? Did he give some great statement of insight? Did he perform a miracle? No, he called Mary by name — "Mary, Mary." And then Mary recognized him. Jesus met Mary at her darkest hour and called her by name.

Paul Zahl, an Episcopal priest in Charleston, South Carolina, once wrote a brilliant statement: "God raises us up by meeting us at the bottom." I believe that. I don't know how dark your life is right now. Perhaps you think you are so low and dark that God could never reach you. Oh, you are mistaken. God is there with you. Just like the Lord found Mary in the dark and called her by name, God can reach you and call you by name. You can never go so low that God cannot find you and raise you up. God can pull you up from whatever is dragging you down.

Michael Brown talked about a true story from one of his favorite writers, Walter Kennicutt. "Kennicutt wrote of accompanying a group of young adults to a county jail to host a worship service. Before the service, they walked the halls of the jail distributing things like soap and toothpaste and other toiletries to the inmates. As they passed by one cell, the man behind the bars shouted obscenities at them. He also said, 'I challenge you to show me one thing Jesus could ever do for my life.'

"Kennicutt was not sure how to respond and felt that no response at all probably made the most sense. Several of the young people in the group were obviously frightened, and he just wanted to hurry them along. But, Kennicutt said that he will never forget what happened next. A certain young man in the group slowly walked over to the bars, unbuttoned his sleeve, rolled it up and showed the inmate his arm. "You know how I got those scars, don't you?" the young man said. The inmate didn't answer, but he knew. He knew those were scars from shooting up heroin. The young man rolled his sleeve back down and said: "Jesus got me out of a cell just like yours, and out of a habit that was going to kill me. And that is what he can do for you.'"

What is holding you captive today? Is it a bad job or relationship? Is it a destructive habit? Maybe it is guilt over something you did? Whatever is causing your despair today, I know one thing is for sure — the risen Lord can help you rise above it. Jesus can free you to live the abundant life. This is the message of Easter.

You Can Rise Above Defeat

The first thing Mary saw when she went to the tomb was the stone which had been rolled away. I am sure Mary wondered how a sealed stone that weighed tons could have been rolled away. The gospel of Matthew tells us that it was the power of God through the angels that rolled the stone away.

Whenever I visualize the scene of the rolled away stone it always makes me think of the people I know who remain in tombs of defeat and they can't roll the stone away to free themselves. Some remain in the tomb of their past and they can't get out of it. Some remain in the tomb of a mistake that they will not allow themselves to live down.

What tomb of defeat are you living in? Perhaps you are living in a tomb and you have said so many times, "I have tried to roll away the stone, but I can't do it by myself! It is too heavy."

The good news of Easter is that you don't have to roll the stone away by yourself. There is a power available to you that can empower you to roll that stone away and be free forever. That power is the resurrection power of Jesus Christ.

French scientist and mystic Theilhard de Chardin once said, "We are not human beings having a spiritual experience. We are spiritual beings having a human experience." How true. We have the Spirit of God available to us to help us rise above defeat.

What does it really mean to believe in Easter? In the Bible, the words "believe in" or "trust in" can mean "to lean your whole weight upon."

James Moore loved to tell the story about the great pianist Ignace Paderewski. Paderewski was Poland's most famous pianist and prime minister. During his long and illustrious career, Paderewski scheduled a concert in a small village to cultivate the arts in Poland. A young mother bought tickets for the Paderewski performance. Her young son had just started taking piano lessons, and she wanted to expose him to one of the greatest piano players in the world.

When the night arrived, they found their seats near the front of the concert hall. The mother spotted a friend nearby and began to chat. As she turned back from her visit, she was stunned to see that her little boy was not in his seat. He had slipped out of sight. Just then the house lights came down and the spotlight came up. It was at that moment that everyone knew where the little ten-year-old boy had run off to. He was seated at the concert piano on stage innocently picking out "Twinkle, Twinkle, Little Star."

His mother was mortified. The stagehands ran out to grab the boy, but suddenly Paderewski appeared on stage and waved them away. Paderewski quickly moved to the piano and standing behind the little boy, he whispered into his ear, "Don't quit! Keep playing! Don't stop!" Leaning over, Paderewski reached down with his left hand and began filling in the bass part. Soon his right arm reached around the other side of the boy, and he played another part. Together, the old master and the young novice mesmerized the crowd with beautiful music. They did it together (Moore, "Rise Above It").

You know what Easter is all about? Easter is about the risen Lord coming alongside of you and whispering in your ear, "Don't quit on life. Don't quit on yourself. Don't give up on me. I'm here to help you rise above anything. Put your trust in me. Lean your whole weight on me. We will do it together." You can rise above discouragement. You can rise above despair. You can rise above defeat. Easter means you can rise above it. I believe that. Do you believe it?

Amen.

James Moore's Easter sermon "Rise Above It" was a helpful resource for me as I prepared this message.

Second Sunday of Easter
John 20:19-31

Faith Is An Inside Job

If you've ever doubted God's existence or know someone who has, this message is for you. If you are afraid to express your struggles with faith, this message is for you. The truth is 99 % of us are in one of those categories, and the 1% is lying! So this message is for everyone!

I have gone through seasons of doubt. It's called being human. It is normal. I wouldn't be much of preacher if I didn't struggle with doubt. I wouldn't have much to offer you. I believe with Frederick Buechner that "doubts are the ants in the pants of faith; they keep it alive and moving."

There is more faith in doubt than you might think. John Wesley said that doubt is the front porch to faith. You show me someone who has never gone through seasons of doubt and I'll show you someone with a shallow faith.

I'd like to share some insights I have learned in my struggles with doubt, and I hope they can help you. If you open your heart to today's message you may begin to doubt your doubts and experience the power of faith.

Here's a question: Why can't God do something spectacular for those who doubt him? "God, if you exist give me a hole in one on this next golf hole!" Why can't God just sky write a message in the sky that says, "I love you, God." Or how about God doing a world tour, appearing in every city with a message for the world: "I do exist!"

Ever wondered why God doesn't do something spectacular like that? It would remove all of our doubts and silence skeptics and cynics.

When British philosopher Bertrand Russell was asked what he would say if after death he found himself confronted by God. Russell replied, "I would say, 'Why didn't you prove yourself to those who doubted you?'"

A clever comedian once said that he would have no difficulty believing in God. "All God would have to do would be to deposit $1,000,000 in my bank account."

Unfortunately, for whatever reason, God does not operate that way. There is an old saying, "If there is a God he is the ultimate under achiever." But is he really? Has God really left us with no evidence or proof that he exists?

When I think about the moment my son Paul was born or when I look at a sunset, or gaze at the stars, I ask "What more proof of God do we need than that?" All we have to do is look at the glory of creation to see that there is a God. Theologians call this the design argument. When we look at wonders around us, we conclude that all of it did not occur by change. There has to be a designer.

However, there are some who are not so sure. I had a friend in college who had a very strong faith. He grew up in a strong Christian home and was very active in his church. He began his freshman year determined to hold on to his faith. He was exposed to new knowledge of science and biology. He also learned from the religion department that there were alternative ways to interpret the Bible and faith. It wasn't long before many doubts crept in. These doubts led him to give up his faith. Today he has embraced the faith again and is active in a church but he still has many doubts and questions.

My friend reminded me of the man who came to Jesus with his sick boy in the gospel of Mark. He said to Jesus, "I believe; help my unbelief." If we are honest, that's where most of us live. Most of us live on top of that semicolon between belief and unbelief. There are days when we feel like Jesus is holding our hand and there are days we feel completely in the dark.

If you struggle with doubts and questions about God's existence you're in good company. The Bible is filled with people who doubted God. One of the famous doubters in scripture doubted so much that doubting became his first name — "Doubting" Thomas. His signature scene appears in chapter 20 of John. Appearances of the resurrected Jesus were happening everywhere. Most of the disciples had encountered him, but not Thomas. Here is what Thomas had to say about that:

> *But Thomas (who was called the Twin), one of the twelve, was not with them when Jesus came. So the other disciples told him, "We have seen the Lord." But he said to them, "Unless I see the mark of the nails in his hands, and put my finger in the mark of the nails and my hand in his side, I will not believe." – John 20:24-25*

At one time or another we have felt like Thomas: "Unless I see in his hands the print of the nails, and place my finger in the mark of the nails, and place my hand in his side, I will not believe." Maybe today you wish God would just prove himself in some way.

Thomas got his wish. Take a look:

> *A week later his disciples were again in the house, and Thomas was with them. Although the doors were shut, Jesus came and stood among them and said, "Peace be with you." Then he said to Thomas, "Put your finger here and see my hands. Reach out your hand and put it in my side. Do not doubt but believe." Thomas answered him, "My Lord and my God!" — John 20:26-28*

Wouldn't you love to have that experience? "Finally! He showed up. I see proof with my own eyes. Now I believe!" But notice what Jesus said next:

> *Jesus said to him, "Have you believed because you have seen me? Blessed are those who have not seen and yet have come to believe." — John 20:29*

Why would Jesus make that statement? "Blessed are those who have not seen and yet have come to believe." It would make more sense if Jesus had said, "How noble and amazing are those who come to believe without proof." But that is not what he said. He said they were "blessed." Why would those who believe without proof be blessed? Because experiencing God goes much deeper than experiencing proof. It is beyond the physical. Those who experience God beyond what can be seen by the eyes are truly blessed because they experience God on a deeper level.

God is a not a science experiment. God is a personal being. God is not an object to be observed; God is a spiritual power to be experienced. How do I know that? Well, let me share a few reasons why I believe this:

Proof Of God Doesn't Guarantee Belief In God

It's impossible for God to prove his existence. Why? Because God gave us freedom of thought. Anything God could or would do to prove his existence would be refuted or explained away. For example, say God did send a comet in the sky to write to the world, "I love you, God." Or say God toured the world like Elvis and gave a show filled with miracles and wonders. You would still have folks who would not believe there is God. Instead they would say:

"-The people witnessing the demonstration were hallucinating or dreaming
-The demonstration was an optical illusion or a freak occurrence of atmospheric conditions
-The demonstration is natural phenomena which science will eventually explain
-The demonstration was not caused by God, but by someone else, possibly someone masquerading as God
-The demonstration was misinterpreted: aliens made a mistake when they tried to contact us, the scientists who documented it made mistakes or were biased towards theism, etc." (https:// www.rational-christianity.net/proof.html).

Regardless of what God tried to do to prove his existence, some folks would still find some way to refute it. So proof of God doesn't always guarantee a belief in God.

Proof Does Not Always Lead To Faith
Many make the assumption that if God showed up and proved he existed to everyone then all would be right with the world. Your Uncle Billy would stop drinking and come to church. Your atheist friend would convert and become a preacher. Sorry to burst your bubble, but proof of God does not always lead to faith in God. The Bible says, "Even the demons believe and tremble."

We must remember that there were many people in the Bible who witnessed miracles but did not follow God. Countless people witnessed the miracles of Jesus and yet fell away when things got tough.

I like how rationalchritianity.net puts it: "Even if God provided proof that was satisfactory to everyone, faith and trust would still be required to follow God. The atheist's question would merely change from 'Why doesn't God prove his existence?' to 'Why doesn't God explain why he did this and not that?' Atheists themselves might come to believe in a higher power, but not all of them would become Christians: one can believe God exists without believing he's worthy of worship, or that Christ saved us from sin" (https:// www.rational-christianity.net/proof.html).

Faith Is An Inside Job

A relationship with God must take place on a spiritual level. It can't happen on the outside of you. It must happen on the inside. Faith is an inside job. God communicates to us personally and intimately. God relates to each of us individually.

In his sermon, "Learning to Doubt our Doubts," King Duncan wrote, "This means you cannot find God with the most powerful telescope ever built. You cannot find him with a slide rule, or a test tube, or an enormous computer. There is only one way to find God and that is to take a step of faith, entrust your life to him. Could I prove to you that love exists? A scientist could attach electrodes to the skin of a person in love and measure the pulse, the respiration and the blood pressure of a person in the presence of their beloved. But that would not prove love. Too much caffeine that morning at breakfast might cause the same bodily reactions. The only way you and I can ever prove love is to experience it — to love and be loved" (sermons.com).

So it is with faith and experiencing God. The only way to truly existence the reality of God is by trusting him with your life and developing a relationship with him. The reality of God begins with an intimate connection with him and his love. The prophet Jeremiah puts it this way: When you search for me, you will find me; if you seek me with all your heart" (Jeremiah 29:13).

A relationship with God must be based on trust, not proof. *Belief in God based on proof is a science experiment. Faith in God based on trust is a relationship.*

Maybe this is starting to make sense but you still have your doubts and you don't know what to do with them. Let me lift up a passage of scripture for you from the gospel of John, chapter 6. People are hearing Jesus teach and preach and they find his teachings difficult. More and more people are leaving him. It was fun for a while — healings and miracles. Then Jesus started getting more challenging in his teachings and doubt crept in. Verse 66 says, "Because of this many of his disciples turned back and no longer went about with him."

There were doubts, struggles, and questions by many and some decided not to follow Jesus anymore. Sometimes doubts can do that to people. They allow their doubt to take over their lives and they stop believing in God. They become bitter about the church and religion. And that is where you may be today and that's okay. God still believes in you even if you don't believe in him. But watch what happens next.

So Jesus asked the twelve, "Do you also wish to go away?"
– John 6:67

Jesus saw everyone deserting him and he turned to the twelve and said, "Everyone's leaving me. What about you? You want to leave me too?" Simon Peter replied with the wisest answer anyone could give:

Lord, to whom can we go? You have the words of eternal life.
– John 6:68

Sit with Peter's response for just a moment. Here is what I believe was going on inside the heart of Peter. When everyone else had chosen to walk away from Jesus, he thought about leaving too. I am sure he had his doubts. But perhaps he began to ask, "Where are they going? Who or what are they going to follow? What are they going to put their hope in? What are they going to put their trust in? Who are they going to put their faith in? In themselves? In others? In the Roman government? In pleasures?

Jesus was the only one who could hold water! He was the only one I could really lean on! Peter said, "Lord, where else can I go? Where else can we go? You have the words to life. There is only you! I may have questions and doubts but there is only you."

When I have gone through periods of doubt and questioning I remember Peter's words, "Where else can I go?" I can't go to anyone else! Who else can give me life?

The key question in the midst of doubt is "Who or what will I follow?" Think that through. Doubt God, struggle, get angry, search. It is good for you. But before you make the ultimate decision to abandon your faith, ask to whom or what will you go? Think about that. What is really going to satisfy you? What is really going to help you discover the truth about your life? What is really going to give you meaning? There is only God. He is the answer to all your questions and doubts. "To whom can you go?"

A cynical young medical student confronted a pastor: "I have dissected the human body," he announced, "and I found no soul." The pastor said, "That's interesting. When you dissected the brain did you find a thought? When you dissected the eye did you find vision? When you dissected the heart did you find love?" The student answered thoughtfully, "No, I did not." The pastor replied gently, "Of course you believe in the existence of thoughts, of vision, and of love. The human soul is the totality of man's existence in relationship with God. Just because you cannot locate it on a medical chart does not mean that it does not exist" (source: "Frustrated by Lack of Faith" by King Duncan).

When we stop searching for proof of God on the outside and begin to seek an experience of God on the inside, we will find all the proof we need.

Amen.

Third Sunday of Easter
John 21:1-19

When You're Out Of Answers

An old legend tells how a man once stumbled upon a great red barn after wandering for days in a forest in the dark. He was seeking refuge from a terrible storm. He went inside the barn and his eyes grew accustomed to the darkness. He was shocked to discover that this was the barn where the devil kept his storehouse of seeds. They were the seeds that were sown in the hearts of humans.

The man became curious and lit a match. He began exploring the piles of bins of seeds round him. He observed that the greatest majority of them said, "Seeds of Discouragement."

About that time one of the devil's helpers arrived to pick up a load of seeds. The man asked him, "Why the abundance of discouragement seeds?" The helper laughed and replied, "Because they are so effective and they take root so quickly."

He was right. Discouragement is an evil and insidious tool. There is nothing more hopeless or helpless than feeling discouraged. A discouraged person can easily turn into a defeated person. And once a person believes they are defeated, well, God help them.

I imagine many of you who are in the same boat. You look failure in the face day after day and it feels impossible to believe that anything will ever change. Life has come to a halt. You don't know how to get out of this slump that seems to be taking over your life.

Maybe it is a failing marriage, a personal dysfunction of some kind, poor performance at work or in sports. Maybe it is a shattered dream or a life goal that seems unattainable. Perhaps it is a personal demon that haunts you and nothing you do will make it go away. Or maybe it is a crisis of faith. You are so burned out and hardened that you just don't know if you have the strength to believe and live out your faith anymore.

Today, I want to offer a word that I believe has to potential to help you get out from under your failures. I believe today's message will not only help you start to believe that failure is never final but it just might provide the answer you need to succeed.

Today's gospel lesson is about three discouraged men who encountered Jesus. Jesus said something to these unhappy men that transformed them. Their disappointment turned into delight.

These three men in our text were real fishermen; not just a bunch of buddies drinking beer on a chartered boat trying to catch marlin. These men were workers whose families went hungry if they didn't catch any fish.

They had worked for hours and had zilch. Nothing. That's why I am sure Simon was a bit irritated when Jesus confidently said, "Well, go out into the deeper water over there and let down your nets and see what happens."

I can just imagine Simon thinking, "Buddy, you may know the Bible, you may know how to preach, but you are not a fisherman. I am. I know what I am doing, so don't talk to me about fishing. You sound ridiculous."

But wisely, Simon didn't say that. Instead he said, "It won't do any good. We've worked all night, and don't have a single fish to show for it."

Ever been there? I have. Maybe many of you are there right now. The harder you try the worse it gets. The more you work the more you fail.

That's how Simon felt. So probably out of frustration and the urge to prove Jesus wrong, Simon said to Jesus, "Okay, if you say so. We will drop our nets where you said, but don't be surprised when we don't catch anything."

Well, you know the story. They caught so many fish that their nets were breaking! Simon needed his buddies from another boat to help him haul in all the fish.

What is the lesson? If nothing is going well for you, if you continue to fail, if you feel hopeless and discouraged, perhaps the waters you have been working are too shallow. Charles Bayer reminds us that sometimes the answer we are looking for lies in deeper waters, to places we have never gone. Sometimes we have to take a risk. And I know it might scare you to death. But isn't it worth a shot? (Bayer, "When Your Nets Are Empty")

I took a chance in deeper waters when I asked my wife Brandy out for a date many years ago. She was way out of my league. She still is. But, by the grace of God, she married me and is still with me.

If your nets are empty, take a risk and do something different. Venture out into deeper waters. Think outside the box. Try that crazy idea. It just might work.

You see, if we are fishing in barren waters, and somebody tells us to do something different, getting upset won't solve the problem. Giving all these reasons and excuses why we can't do it won't solve the problem. Staying in our shallow comfort zones won't solve the problem. We can either keep doing what we have always been doing and moan and complain or we can do something different. It is up to us.

Bill Self used to talk about taking his grandkids to the pool and observing that all of the noise came from the shallow end of the pool. The same is true in the church and in life in general. All the noise and complaining usually comes from those who are too preoccupied with all their excuses why they can't go into deeper waters. Those in the deep end are too preoccupied with growing and doing something meaningful to bother with making noise and excuses.

Bayer put it this way: "I know people who are miserable and unsatisfied because for years they have refused to leave shallow waters. They refuse to risk anything. They have resources but do not use them, skills but do not develop them, dreams but do not follow them, gifts but do not share them, possessions but do not dedicate them because they are afraid that to do anything, give anything, risk anything is too much of a threat. So, they just sit and pout in the middle of their boat, in the shallow waters, where there are no fish, and complain, are dissatisfied, bored and wonder why nothing happens. And then we wonder why their nets are empty." ("When Your Nets are Empty")

They are empty because they have not ventured into deeper waters. They are empty because they have not risked anything. They are empty because they refuse to change.

Peter, James, and John not only ventured into deeper waters with their boat, but also with their faith. This led to serious changes. They realized they had a larger purpose, and they left everything to follow Jesus. They walked away from the biggest day in their lives and they never looked back.

Maybe your net, your life is empty, and your failure is that you can't find fulfillment. You keep thinking you will find life and happiness in the shallowness of worldly pleasures. For you, going into deeper waters means making the decision to follow Christ as your Lord and Savior.

This applies to those of us who are veterans of the faith too. Maybe you feel empty spiritually. Maybe it is time to go into deeper waters with Christ. As Howard Olds said, "Some of us have stepped into the kiddie pool of God's grace, but have yet to experience the thrill of diving deeper. We've gotten our feet wet, but have not yet known the joy of having our souls soaked." We don't know the joy of going deeper with Christ and like those at the shallow end, we just make a lot of noise that simply reflects our unwillingness to take a risk for Christ and dive deeper.

Today's question for each of us is: Into what deeper waters is Christ calling you? The answer you are looking for today just might be in how you answer that question.

This is also the question for us as a church. I often wonder where Jesus will tell us to lower our nets next. Will we do it? Will we be the church Christ calls us to be?

Truly following Jesus means going into deeper waters, taking new paths, taking risks. This is when we find the joy and the answers we are looking for.

Linda Clare learned this and discovered something she would never forget. Linda was spending long hours as a day care provider and thought, "I wonder if there is more to life than baby-sitting." She decided to venture into deeper waters and teach a few of her kids about her faith and how to pray. She wasn't sure what difference it was making until a father came in to pick up his toddler one day and said, "I want to thank you for teaching Kasey how to pray. She says grace at home every night now and we are becoming used to it. We are now trying to find a church because Kasey is insisting." Linda ventured into deeper waters with Christ and look what happened.

Author and educator Howard Hendricks was on a plane one day that was delayed from takeoff. As passengers became irritated and demanding, Howard noticed how gracious and kind one of the flight attendants was to the passengers. When they were finally in the air he continued to be amazed at her attitude. When she came by his seat, Howard asked if he could write a letter to the airline about her exceptional kindness. "I don't work for the airline," she replied, "I work for Jesus Christ. My husband and I prayed this morning that I would be a good representative of Jesus Christ on this flight." That lady ventured looked past all the noise and ventured into deeper waters with her faith.

Are you discouraged? Do you feel empty? Do you feel hopeless. "Put out into the deep and let down your nets for a catch" and just see what happens.

Amen.

How Much Faith Is Enough?

Rodin was a famous French sculptor who is considered the pioneer of modern sculpture. The story is told that one day Rodin saw a huge, carved crucifix beside a road. He immediately loved the artwork and insisted on having it for himself. He purchased the cross and arranged to have it delivered to his house. Unfortunately, it was too big for the building. So, of all things, he knocked out the walls, raised the roof, and rebuilt his home around the cross.

That's the thing about Jesus. He's just too big to be contained by our modern lifestyles and philosophies. Very rarely does his message fit in with how we think life should operate. This does not mean we haven't tried to cram him in to our culture. Oh we have. Over the years, authors, spiritual gurus, motivational speakers, celebrities, moralistic salesmen, and even preachers have tried really hard to make Jesus fit into the comfortable houses we have built. Sports figures have said that if Jesus did ministry today he would be the greatest quarterback. Businessmen say he would be the greatest CEO or salesman. Even ministers who see themselves as being on the cutting edge of ministry say Jesus would be the greatest visionary leader and would be lead pastor of a mega church. We have tried to fit Jesus into all kinds of categories that affirm the way we live.

The only problem is that if we actually start reading the New Testament and look at what he really said and did, we find that he does not fit into any of our comfortable categories. In fact, most often he obliterates our categories and embodies a radical message that is intended to transform us into his disciples. We find that we have to rebuild our lives so that he can fit.

And let's be honest, most folks don't want to hear that. We don't want to hear that we must rearrange our lives and priorities around Jesus. Most want Jesus on their own terms.

Peter Gomes, the insightful preacher of Harvard University's Memorial Church, tells of a famous cartoon that appeared in *New Yorker* magazine. The cartoon shows a well-dressed couple leaving church after saying nice things to the preacher at the door. The wife, covered in furs and jewels, says to her well to do husband, "It can't be easy for him not to offend us."

I laughed out loud when I read about that cartoon, and I laughed because of the truth of it. It is rather funny when I think of what I do up here every Sunday. My job is to preach the gospel. That sounds nice, it sounds good. That is what you expect me to do, and that is what God has called me to do. But when I read the gospels that contain the gospel teachings of Jesus I realize once again how dangerous my job really is. Because the gospel is not meant to confirm; it is meant to confront and that is dangerous business. Who likes confrontation?

Let's face it. Most people do not go to church to be confronted with the gap between who they are and what the gospel calls them to be. Most people come to church because they crave confirmation of the status quo, of what they already believe, of what they are already doing. This fact sometimes spoils the good feelings I get when folks compliment my sermons. I am human like the rest of you, and it feels good to receive compliments. I recall recently someone telling me how much they liked a sermon I preached. I asked, "What did you like about it?" They replied, "I agreed with it." And so it is.

The only problem is that we don't find many people complimenting Jesus' preaching or agreeing with it. In fact, the first time Jesus got up to preach in his hometown, he almost got killed. The people he grew up with were so offended they tried to throw him off a cliff! How's that for sermon feedback? Jesus had a knack for rubbing people the wrong way.

For example, a desperate man once ran to Jesus in the midst of his disciples and a big crowd, knelt before him and said, "Lord, have mercy on me. My son has epilepsy, and suffers terribly. I brought him to your disciples and they couldn't help. Please help me."

What did Jesus say? He didn't say, "There, there." He didn't hug the man and tell him everything is going to be all right. What did he do? He took the opportunity to insult his disciples. "Are you kidding? You faithless and perverse generation! How long do I have to put up with you? How long do I have to deal with you? Bring him here." And then he healed the boy. I can hear John whispering to Peter in the background, "I think Jesus needs to work on his people skills."

Well, the disciples had egg on their faces. After the crowd left, the disciples asked Jesus, "Why couldn't we heal the boy like you?" Jesus replied, "Because your faith is small. You have so little faith. If you have faith as small as a mustard seed you can move mountains. Nothing will be impossible to you." And the disciples must have looked at each other in amazement and said, "Is he serious?"

I must admit that I feel sorry for the disciples. I see them running after Jesus as he taught, preached. and healed, taking notes on what he said and did. I see them conferring with each other on what they thought he meant when said this or said that. I see them scratching their heads and sometimes shaking their heads in astonishment. But if I had been one of the disciples this little incident with Jesus would have sent me to a boil. "Here I am. I left my job and family to follow this guy. I try to understand everything he says and do everything he tells me to do. Then he embarrasses me in front of this crowd, and then he tells me my faith is small?"

I imagine the religious people who approached Jesus in our assigned text in John 10 felt the same way when Jesus called them out for not believing. He said that he told them who he was and he backed it up with his works, but they still did not believe.

I wonder how much faith and belief Jesus requires. How much faith is enough?

I once knew a couple in another church I served who had a very sick daughter. They tried everything to help her. They went to all kinds of doctors. They went to all kinds of specialists. They had her on every prayer list you could think of. They prayed for help and guidance every day. Nothing worked. They were so desperate that they took her to a famous faith healer. He tried to heal her, but he couldn't. When they asked him why, he said to the couple, "You just don't have enough faith."

There was a minister who tried to start a new church. He was filled with vim and vigor. He planned well and strategized well. He had people praying for him. For two years he preached his heart out, pastored his heart out, but the church never grew. It had the same twenty people coming that it had started with. The denomination behind him pulled the plug. When he met with his supervisor, the supervisor said to him, "This new church start should have never failed. You need to evaluate your faith."

Is this really what Jesus is trying to tell us? That if we can't seem to pick a mountain and move it, it is because we don't have enough faith? That if we can't seem to overcome an obstacle we don't have enough faith? That when we fail it is because we don't have enough faith? Really? I mean, my theological training won't allow for such an explanation. We can't explain a lack of faith on everything. This is a sinful world, so bad things happen. Sometimes circumstances are beyond our control. Sometimes life throws us things that cannot be resolved by simple faith.

This is a complicated world that requires more than religious pablum. If you want something done, you have to work for it. If you want a problem solved, you have to save, plan, strategize. If you want to accomplish something, you have to have the skills and talent to do it. If you want to change the world, you need money and resources to do it. We could do without the answers of the self-help coaches and religious gurus telling us it is about belief and faith.

Yet here we are in church with a Bible on our altar, a Bible here in the pulpit, that says over and over that faith is essential. Here we are showing support of scripture that says, "Without faith it is impossible to please God;" "The just shall live by faith." Here we are believing in a man who said, "Your faith has saved you. Your faith has made you well. O ye of little faith. Where is your faith?" And, of course, "If you have faith you can move mountains, nothing will be impossible to you!"

Do we really believe it is that simple? Well, maybe on Sunday mornings we believe that. But when we go back to school, work, or our regular routines on Monday, it is hard for us to live by faith. The just may live by faith, but most of us live as if the smart live by an agenda.

There they were in a church meeting planning a new ministry. They had some of the smartest people in the congregation gathered around a big table for three or four hours. Everyone was teeming with fresh insights and creative ideas. It was exciting. They had a timeline planned out. They had their goals to meet written out on a white board. This was going to revolutionize how the church would do ministry. They were ready to adjourn the meeting. Then a member of the youth group who had been quiet the whole meeting raised her hand and said, "Don't you think we need to pray about all of this? We forgot to pray at the beginning of the meeting. At youth we always pray before our meetings." The leader of the meeting said, "Good idea. Bow your heads. Let's say a quick prayer. It's late."

They were in a budget meeting. You know how budget meetings are. They had their work cut out for them. They discussed and argued all night. "Where are we going to find the money? How will we raise the money? What are we going to do?" Then someone had the audacity to mumble something about faith. Then there was the reply, "Well, the church is a business just like anything else."

Controversy had hit the church hard. There were rumors spreading all over the place. Many people had left the church in disgust. "Too much change in too little time" people would say. The pastor was angry at this group. This group was angry at that group. The denominational powers that be called a meeting to hear everyone out to help bring peace and resolution to this conflict. One influential man got up and complained about leadership and decisions that were made, and all the changes. Then he ended his rousing speech with, "Not in my church! Not in my church!" And many people applauded. Would it surprise you to know that the name Jesus or the word prayer was never mentioned in that meeting?

Faith seems really simple. Faith seems really easy. But the truth of the matter is faith is really hard. That's probably why we find Jesus' words today so offensive, so outrageous. Faith in hard work — you bet. Faith in our best made plans — absolutely. Faith in what we can see — sure. Faith in our resources and money going to where we think it should go — yes. Faith in our agenda — of course. But faith in something beyond our control, faith in a God who is bigger than us, faith in a power that is greater than our agenda, huh well, let me get back to you on that.

God's not bad when you are in trouble or you have exhausted every resource, but putting God in charge of your life, of your decisions, of your resources, of your money, that's for the fanatics. I guess that is right. It takes a fanatic to believe in Jesus because Jesus was a fanatic. He was fanatical enough to have faith in God.

I remember meeting a person with faith. He was one of those people that seemed to live his life and ministry with very little effort. Everything he touched turned to gold. I shared the platform with him one time at a speaking engagement. He had overcome obstacle after obstacle in his life to get where he was. He was extremely successful in what he did. I had never heard a person like him before or knew someone who touched people the way he touched people. I must say I was very curious about what made him tick, and what made him so successful and effective. I told him that I would like to join him for lunch and pick his brain. We got our food and sat down at the table.

I had my questions. Where did he go to school? Where did he go to church? Who were his mentors? What was his secret? He said, "Can we pray for our meal, first?" "Right, right, of course. Sorry. I forgot." He took my hand and squeezed it, and you know what he said? You know what he prayed? I couldn't believe it. It was the simplest prayer. One I heard a million times, but I had forgotten. He prayed, "Not my will, Lord, but yours be done. Amen."

Amen.

Fifth Sunday of Easter
John 13:31-35

Where Is The Love?

When I was in college, I went to a pool party. I remember it being pretty tame by college standards. The parents of the home were there! I remember the dad of the house being a really funny guy. We joked around, laughed and carried on.

Later in the evening, we were sitting by the pool and the father asked me what my major was. I told him it was religion. He laughed and said, "Yeah, right." I said, "No, I'm serious. It is religion." He asked, "Why religion?" I told him I was going to be a preacher." He said, "A what? You don't seem like any preacher I know (I took that as a compliment). You laugh and joke and have fun. You seem normal."

Before I left the party he said something to me I will never forget: "I'm in my fifties and you are the first Christian I've ever met that I enjoyed being around."

I don't tell you that story because I'm the hero because believe me I'm not usually the hero of my stories! I share it because that man at the party is not alone. There are many people who have never had a positive experience of Christians.

Oliver Wendell Holmes once said, "I might have entered the ministry if certain clergymen I knew had not looked and acted so much like undertakers."

Robert Louis Stevenson once entered in his diary, as if he was recording an extraordinary phenomenon, "I have been to church today, and am not depressed!"

Ghandi was famous for saying, "I like your Christ. It is Christians I have a problem with."

Over the years, Christianity has lost its fascination because it looks less and less like Jesus.

Sadly, when many of your friends, co-workers and neighbors think of Christians they don't think of Jesus, love, or kindness. They think of people who are judgmental, opinionated and hypocritical. Are we surprised there are so many empty pews in churches?

As a Christian, have you ever thought about the kind of impression you make on others? What words would people use to describe you?

Jesus is clear about the impression he wants us to make in this world. In Mark, when Jesus was questioned about the supreme commandment of the faith he replied, *"Love the Lord your God with all your heart and with all your soul and with all your mind and with all your strength.' The second is this: 'Love your neighbor as yourself.' There is no commandment greater than these."* — Mark 12:30-31

Notice the key word is love. What was most important to Jesus had nothing to do with theology, biblical interpretation, or rules to follow. It had everything to do with how well we love.

I believe that's what Jesus had in mind when he commanded, *"Let your light shine before others, that they may see your good deeds and glorify your Father in heaven."* — Matthew 5:16

Imagine if every Christian in this world (that's 2.2 billion people, over 30% of the world's population) got up every day, read these verses and said, "Today I am going to let my love light shine. Today everything I think, say and do will reflect the greatest commandment." Can you imagine? It would be a different world!

Unfortunately, many Christians hide their lights under a bushel by favoring judgment over grace, hate over love, rules over relationships, dogma over forgiveness, and despair over hope.

Many years ago, while serving another church an angry lady came to see me. She sat down in my office and said, "I have problems with your sermons." I replied, "And what is that?" She said, "You preach on love too much!" I replied, "Come again? Before we go any further I want to suggest that you never repeat that. You will not come across well to others." That did not go over very well. But she was not deterred.

She continued, "You preach on love too much. Where is the judgment? Where is talk about sin?" I responded, "Well, I believe those subjects deserve attention, but last time I checked Jesus said that the world will know we are his disciples not by our judgment or self-righteousness, but by our love for one another."

I'd like to tell you that she had a change of heart. But she didn't. She left my officer angrier than when she came in. Sitting in judgment was more important to her than it was to Jesus.

Jesus didn't say let your judgment and opinions shine so that no one in the right mind would want to be a Christian.

Unfortunately, that is often the reality. Too many Christians are known by their opinions than by their love for others.

Bob Goff said, "Only Jesus has the power to change people, and it will be harder for them to see Jesus if their view of him is blocked by our big opinions."

When we uncover our light by removing our judgments and opinions we will be a lot more attractive to the world. Believe me, there is nothing more attractive than the gospel. Our message is the most attractive message in the world! God created us, loves us, redeemed us and wants a relationship with us.

The late Aretha Franklin understood the attractiveness of God's light and love. She once said, "When God loves you, what can be better than that?" She was right. There is nothing better than that.

But there are a lot of people who don't know that love — who don't know they are loved. This is a cold and dark world filled with people who are desperate for our light. Many are wondering if the violence and evil around us is all there is.

Are you letting your love light shine? This beat up world is watching us wondering if our faith is genuine. If not, why should they bother with our faith? They don't expect us to be perfect, but they do expect to see some evidence that the love of Christ is real. And how can they know unless we let it shine?

Either we believe Jesus Christ is the help and hope of the world or we don't. Either we believe Jesus is the light of the world or we don't. Either we believe the light of Christ is within us or we don't.

I like the movie *The Incredibles*. It's about a family of superheroes who try to save the world from total destruction. In Bob Goff's book "Love Does," he wrote about the superhero dad in the movie. He is an insurance claims adjustor, but he really wants to use his superhero powers. He begins drawing pictures of the superhero suits he wants to wear. Of course, all the suits he thinks of include capes.

The dad had a friend named Edna who made superhero suits and she kept telling him that he needed to lose the cape. She told him how in the end capes cause big problems for superheroes. They get caught on things like a jet engine or worse and cause big issues. Edna said in the movie, "No capes!" You get a lot more stuff done if you lose the cape. Bob Goff thought Jesus agreed and so do I!

You know what I think will draw the world to Christ and leave a good taste in people's mouths about religion? When Christians lose the cape. So many of us who follow Christ do it with a cape representing something — a cape to be noticed by others so they will think we are so good — a cape representing something we are against, an opinions or judgments — a cape symbolizing what denomination we are part of or our views on a political issue or how we interpret the Bible. Soon we become known by our capes and not by Jesus. Our capes hide our light (Bob Goff, *Love Does*, Nashville, Thomas Nelson Publishers, 2012, p. 159).

Another problem is that if we go around serving Jesus with capes, they eventually get snagged on something — our pride, other people's feelings, people's perceptions of those who follow God. Our capes get in the way.

Goff reminded us that Jesus never wore a cape. Jesus hardly ever talked to anyone about what he had done, the way he loved people. He just did it. And all that mattered to him was that God knew it. When we lose the cape, we don't get confused about what our purpose is, which is to love. We don't forget that it is God who is making things happen. All our energy is channeled into doing great things for God and loving the world like crazy (Goff).

Let's lose the cape as Christians and just go out and share the light and love of Jesus. When we serve Jesus without a cape people will want to know more about Jesus.

Be the change you want to see in the world! I don't know who said that, but they were spot on. If you prefer, "Let there be peace on earth and let it begin with me!" Lose the cape and let your light shine.

Amen.

Keep The Faith

The photographer for a national magazine was assigned to get photos of a forest fire. Smoke at the scene kept him from getting any pictures and he asked his home office to hire a plane. Arrangements were made and he was told to go to the airport, and a plane would be waiting for him.

When he arrived at the airport, a plane was warming up near the runway. He jumped in with his equipment and yelled, "Let's go! Let's go!" The pilot swung the plane into the wind and they soon were in the air.

"Fly over the north side of the fire," yelled the photographer, "and make three or four low level passes." "Why?" asked the pilot. "Because I'm going to take pictures," cried the photographer. "I'm a photographer and photographers take pictures!" After a pause the pilot said, "You mean you're not the instructor?" They were both in trouble!

Trouble has a way of finding in us in life. Trouble is simply a part of life. If we live in this world, we will face trouble.

I was in high school, and it was a Friday afternoon. I had just returned home from playing tennis. I had made plans earlier that day to go out with my friends. And on my way up to my room my Mom and Dad called me into their bedroom. I walked in and told them that whatever they needed to tell me, it needed to be quick. I was running late. My Dad sat in a chair next to his bed taking off his shoes. My Mom stood beside him. My Dad looked up at me and said, "Son, I just got back from the doctor. I have cancer."

They threw a retirement party for him. They roasted him and presented him with all these awards. He had been with the company for a long time. His proud wife was there by his side. They asked what he was going to do in his retirement. "Travel," he said. The couple went on to tell about all the trips they had planned. They went home a proud and happy couple. The next day his wife collapsed and died.

They were a good family. They planned well. Invested their money. Their adorable kids would be taken care of. Well, Dad was at work.

He got a call from his wife. She said, "Have you seen the news? We've lost it all." You see, they invested with a guy named Madoff.

That's the thing about trouble — it rarely announces itself before it comes. Trouble hardly ever says, "Here I come! Get ready!" We wish it would. At least we could prepare for it, or better yet, we could avoid it altogether. But life doesn't work that way. In fact, you are one of three people today — you are coming out of trouble, you are in the middle of trouble, or you about to get into trouble. That's life.

It is because of this truth that our lives are defined by how we respond to trouble. Think about it. Addicts are defined by their ability to numb themselves to trouble. Criminals act out destructively to trouble. Atheists blame the absence of God for trouble. Narcissistic victims exploit trouble to avoid responsibility. Look at many unhealthy people and you will see lives which have been defined by unhealthy responses to trouble. The late M. Scott Peck, who wrote *The Road Less Traveled*, even went so far as to say that the reason for much human dysfunction is the inability to face trouble.

At the bottom of all unhealthy responses to trouble is one bad word. This word is the enemy to all that brings life and joy and peace and hope. The word is "panic". Panic is the feeling of being out of control. Panic is grabbing anything that makes you feel like you are in control, even if it's unhealthy.

Sound familiar? Maybe you are putting on a good show to others, but inside you are coming apart at the seams. Perhaps your business is failing. Maybe you can't find a job in this economy and the bills are piling up. Maybe your marriage is on the rocks. Maybe you're living between doctor appointments and you are scared to death. Maybe the trouble you are facing is sending you into a panic.

I want you to know something. There is another choice besides panic. You can find peace in the midst of your storm. You can calm the raging tempest inside you. You can find help and hope. The Bible does promise us that we can live with confidence and strength each day, no matter what we face. We can live without fear or dread of what might be coming around the corner. We can have peace within regardless of the storms outside of us. We can laugh in the midst of trouble.

I imagine most of you would like to live life this way. I'm sure many of you are sick and tired of slugging through life, being defined by your pain and suffering. You don't want life to simply consist of surviving the day, waiting for the weekend, or trying to find a few moments of peace. You want life to be more than just avoiding as much trouble as you can. You want your life to be full of joy even in the most trying of circumstances. In short, you want to live on the offensive not on the defensive. You don't want to be a victim; you want to be a victor! Well, guess what? You can have that life! All that is needed is one thing.

Oh, I know people who have this one thing. I walked into a hospital room and saw a lady who had it. She was in her forties dying of breast cancer. Her friends were throwing her a birthday party. There was cake beside her bed, and she had a pink party hat on her head. They were playing music and dancing. I thought, "This is not an appropriate scene for someone who is about to die." The whole scene seemed strange until I saw her face. She had it.

My Dad had it. I would see it when he prayed. As a kid, I would open one eye as he prayed at the dinner table and watch him. He had it.

John Wesley had it. It is what transformed his ministry. He found it at Aldersgate.

Countless others have had it over the years, and it has made all the difference to their lives. It has given them strength to deal with trouble and inspiration to do extraordinary things.

What is it? It goes all the way back to Abraham. Oh, you remember Abraham, right? It all started with him. Because he had it, all the rest of us can have it. He had it when God told him to leave everything he knew, and he didn't know where he was going. He had it when God told him and his wife Sarah they were going to have children, when, huh, they no longer had the resources to procreate. Abraham had it.

You know what it is? It's described all over scripture:

> *Now faith is confidence in what we hope for and assurance about what we do not see. This is what the ancients were commended for.*
> *By faith we understand that the universe was formed at God's command, so that what is seen was not made out of what was visible. – Hebrews 11:1-3*

You see, Christians are not perfect. Christians are not in control. Christians don't have all the answers. Christians are not better than other people. Christians are not folks that can give the perfect theological answer to every question.

Christians are those who have learned, like Abraham, that God can be trusted. God can be trusted to give peace in the midst of the storm. God can be trusted to take what is evil and transform it into something good. God can be trusted to empower you in the midst of trouble. God can be trusted to receive you when you die. God can be trusted! (Reference Hebrews 11, by faith, by faith).

If we don't believe this, we might as well be on the golf course today or at the beach. If we don't believe this then we are just playing church. The church is not some charity organization. The church is not some glorified non-profit. The church is a body of people that believe that Jesus can be trusted.

Do you believe that? Faith is not giving up. It is giving in to the only power that can be trusted. Paul taught us this in Philippians:

> *I have learned to be content, whatever the circumstances may be. I know now how to live when things are difficult and I know how to live when things are prosperous. In general, and in particular, I have learned the secret of facing either poverty or plenty. I am ready for anything through the strength of the one who lives within me. – Philippians 4:11-13*

Paul didn't say the secret was a different set of circumstances. He didn't say the secret was will power. He said the secret was Christ in him! Christ enabled him to be "ready for anything" and made him stronger through the trouble he faced. Jesus is all Paul had and he learned that Jesus was enough.

When you face trouble with the confidence that the spirit of Christ will enable you to overcome it and redeem it you, you won't waste your time and energy relying on anything or anyone else. You know the source to draw strength from. You can be ready for anything. You know you have the strength to face anything and you know you will be stronger whenever you conquer your battles in life.

You see, when trouble in life gets the best of us it is usually because we don't believe Jesus is enough. So we try to find peace and strength in other things and they never work. They simply make us vulnerable to the circumstances we face and our problems overwhelm us. Fear develops when we start believing that everything depends on us. Faith and strength develop when we learn that everything depends on God. It has been said, that "we never know that Jesus is enough until Jesus is all we have left."

I can't think of a greater illustration of this than when Peter went barefoot skiing with Jesus. Well, not exactly, but here is the story:

> Shortly before dawn Jesus went out to them, walking on the lake. When the disciples saw him walking on the lake, they were terrified. "It's a ghost," they said, and cried out in fear. But Jesus immediately said to them: "Take courage! It is I. Don't be afraid."
>
> "Lord, if it's you," Peter replied, "tell me to come to you on the water." "Come," he said.
>
> Then Peter got down out of the boat, walked on the water and came toward Jesus. But when he saw the wind, he was afraid and, beginning to sink, cried out, "Lord, save me!" Immediately Jesus reached out his hand and caught him. "You of little faith," he said, "why did you doubt?"
>
> And when they climbed into the boat, the wind died down. Then those who were in the boat worshiped him, saying, "Truly you are the Son of God." – Matthew 14:25-33

Now a popular way to interpret this text is that Peter started to sink when he took his eyes off Jesus. That's not bad but I think it goes a bit deeper than that. Peter came to the place where he realized that he was powerless over the elements of the storm and he was powerless over gravity. He came to a moment of truth where he knew all he had was Jesus.

The late great spiritual writer Henri Nouwen learned this truth at the circus! Nouwen went to see the German trapeze group "The Flying Rodleighs" perform. He was mesmerized by their breath-taking performance as they flew gracefully through the air.

At the end of the show, he spoke with the leader of the troupe, Rodleigh himself. Nouwen asked him how he was able to perform with such grace and ease so high in the air. Rodleigh responded, "The public might think that I am the great star of the trapeze, but the real star is Joe, my catcher... The secret is that the flyer does nothing and the catcher does everything. When I fly to Joe, I have simply to stretch out my arms and hands and wait for him to catch me. The worst thing the flyer can do is try to catch the catcher. I'm not supposed to catch Joe. It's Joe's task to catch me" (Henri J.M. Nouwen, *The Only Necessary Thing: Living a Prayerful Life* (New York: The Crossroad Publishing Company, 1999), pp.195-196).

When trouble comes, so often we try to grab on to God. We think if we do enough mental gymnastics or enough fanciful praying, we can somehow catch God. It's not our job to catch God. God catches us.

So often when we are in trouble, we are like the man who is drowning who can't be rescued because he won't stop flailing his arms in panic. He prevents himself from being rescued because he won't allow the rescuer to grab hold of him.

The best thing we can do when are in trouble and feel like panicking is to be still and allow God to take hold of us. He will if we will let him.

Robert Louis Stevenson once wrote a story about a storm. In the story, he described a ship caught off a rocky coast threatening death to all on board. When terror among the people was at its worst, one man, more daring than the rest, made a perilous trip up to the captain's house.

When he got there, he saw the captain lashed to his post, with his hands on the wheel and turning the ship little by little into the open sea. When the captain saw the ghastly white, terror-stricken face of the man, he smiled, and the man rushed to the deck below, shouting: "I have seen the face of the captain, and he smiled. All is well." The sight of that captain's smiling face averted panic and converted despair into hope.

If you are in trouble today, hear this: I know the captain. You know the captain. All will be well.

Amen.

Ascension of the Lord
Luke 24:44-53

The Great Omission

As Christians, we only have three things that God requires of us: love God with all of our heart, soul, mind. and strength; love our neighbor as ourselves; and make disciples of Jesus Christ. To make disciples means to be witnesses of Christ in order to bring others into a relationship with Christ.

At the end of Matthew, before Jesus ascended to the Father, Jesus' last words to his followers were not, "Go and find a comfortable church and have covered dish dinners." His last words were not, "Go and sing the songs you like in worship. Jesus didn't say, "Try to do some good every once in a while." Jesus said, *"Go and make disciples!"*

In our assigned text in Luke, Jesus told his disciples that they would receive power to preach repentance and the forgiveness of sins "to all nations."

This is called the "Great Commission," not the "Great Suggestion." The church is the only institution in the world that exists for those outside of it. Unfortunately, many churches don't even see it as a suggestion. Instead, it has become the "Great Omission."

As the church has turned inward over the last thirty or forty years, it has lost sight of its mission to make disciples. This is one of the reasons why the mainline church is struggling to grow. The stats don't look good. The mainline church overall is not replenishing itself with a new generation of disciples. We are not reaching the younger generation. Fewer and fewer churches are bringing even one new person to Christ in one year.

What has happened? Why can't the church today be like the early church? The answer comes through something that AW Tozer said long ago: "If the Holy Spirit was withdrawn from the church today, 95% of what we do would go on and no one would know the difference. If the Holy Spirit had been withdrawn from the New Testament church, 95% of what they did would have stopped, and everybody would know the difference."

In our text, Jesus told the disciples that they would receive Holy Spirit power to live out the Great Commission. But is the Holy Spirit the driving force of the church today? If we are to reclaim the fire of the Spirit the early church had, if we are to share our witness effectively, we must get back to fundamentals — what we believe and what we practice. We must be willing to open ourselves to the movement of the Holy Spirit! That's what the early followers of Christ did! They were not sophisticated people. They hadn't been to seminary. They hadn't read books on church growth and marketing the church. They simply made themselves available to the Holy Spirit. And look what happened in Acts 2, verse 6: "Each one heard them speaking in his own language." Now this was not the gift of glossolalia or speaking in tongues. What happened on the day of Pentecost was that a bunch of people from all over the place, all speaking different languages, all coming from different cultures, heard the gospel in their own language. The good news of the saving love of Jesus Christ was communicated to them! It was clear! The Holy Spirit did it through them because they were simply willing to be used! The Holy Spirit broke through communication barriers and the gospel translated.

Isn't it interesting that with all of our miraculous communication technology we still have communication problems? Isn't it interesting that in spite of our advances in Bible translations and production of gimmicks that people are still turned off by religion and the church? It seems we are good at information but not communication.

Will Willimon wrote a few years ago, "To many outside the church, the church is like a football huddle. You know that something important is being said there, but you can't understand a word of it, and all you can see is their rear ends." Someone else said the church needs to speak some other language than *Christianese*.

How is it that the early church was able to communicate so clearly and we have so much trouble? The answer is revealed through a humorous but painfully true cartoon in "Leadership Journal." The church secretary was holding the phone, hollering to the pastor in the adjoining room. She said, "A man from Ripley's Believe It or Not wants a picture of someone on fire for the Lord. Do we have one?"

Where is our passion and love for God and our passion and love for people? This is what translates! That's what translated at Pentecost and that's what translates today! Believe me, when you forgive when everyone else wants revenge, that translates. When you are loving when everyone else is hateful, that translates. When you don't give up on people when everyone else wants to, that translates.

There is a great debate in the church right now on how to be relevant in this post-modern world. Because the mainline church is struggling to grow, we are falling all over ourselves trying to reach the next generation. I went a meeting the other day about this very thing. We talked about gimmicks, models, and strategies. There is a place for all that, but sometimes I wonder with Howard Olds that we are trying so hard to be "with it" that we just "don't get it." We need to be in touch with the world, not in sync with the world.

The church ought to be a little strange. We ought to be a little off-kilter. If people come to the church because the values of the world have diminished them and they are looking for something different, why would they be attracted to us if we are like the world? If we are a little odd, a little weird, that's good. It is as if we are saying, "What you are looking for, you will not find in the world!" People respond to real people who have a real love and passion for God! The gospel does not have to be dressed up, dolled up, souped up, or given a make-over. The gospel does fine by itself.

The early church knew this. The power of the early church was rooted in prayer and discernment from the Holy Spirit. If the church today made itself more available to the power of the Holy Spirit, believe me, people would notice. The church would be led to speak to the real spiritual needs of people. When the church starts doing that, people will listen.

I like the story Wayne Cordeiro tells about a bakery he knew about. It was located in a bad part of town. The bakery was small, rundown, and nondescript. Yet at 5am every morning the aroma of delicious bread emanated from that bakery. People would line up around the block to get their hands on that bread. That is a parable for us as the church. It is not about appearances or gimmicks; it is simply about offering the bread of life. People are so spiritually hungry that all we have to do is offer the bread of life with passion and authenticity, and they will come from all over to taste it.

Does the sweet smell of Christ emanate from your life? Are you sharing your witness? Are you letting your light shine?

The unavoidable truth is that as Christians we are called to testify to the hope that is within us, to tell people about Jesus — to make disciples. Now, this may scare some of you to death. But, take heart and listen closely. By the grace of God, you are able to preach. You don't do it on your own power. This is why Jesus said, "I am with you always, even unto the end of the age." Jesus is always with us, helping us, and empowering us to share the good news. I know he is. As a pastor, I have heard many great sermons from the church. The church is covered in wonderful preachers.

I heard about a woman who had a friend who was an addict. Her addiction was destroying everything she loved. Most people would have said, "Well, we need to pray that she gets the help she needs." But that is not what this woman did. She wrote her friend a letter telling her that she was going to lose everything including her life unless she went into treatment and received the help she needed. And then she wrote in her letter that the only one who could make her whole is Jesus Christ.

Where did she get the power to write a letter like that? Jesus said, "Go and make disciples and I will be with you always."

He was a young man still living at home. He was rather quiet and kept to himself. One day his coworker found him in the restroom crying. His coworker asked him if he could help. The young man confided in him. He told him that his girlfriend was pregnant, and he had just revealed this to his parents the night before. They were very strict and religious. They screamed at him and said that he had embarrassed them. They said he had shamed the family and told him that he should never set foot in their house again.

What did his coworker do? He reached out, put his arm around him and said, "I am sorry that happened to you. I am sure this is difficult for your parents, and I am certain this is difficult for you. But I am a Christian, and I believe that God loves you, and his love will help you through the most difficult situations."

How was that coworker able to say something like that? Jesus said, "Go and make disciples and remember I am with you always."

I remember preaching at a youth camp several years ago. The worship service went really late. I didn't get up to preach until about 11pm. It didn't help that I had the flu. But it was the last service of the week, and I had to finish. I don't know what I said. I was so sick. I was just trying to get through it. I thought it was the worst sermon I ever delivered.

After the service, a teenage girl approached me. She looked very angry. She said, "I have to find out if something is true." I replied,

"What's that?" She said, "You mentioned tonight that God loves me. Do you believe that? I don't believe anyone has ever loved me. My dad left me and my mother abused me, and I moved from one institution to another. I've been sexually abused, neglected, and you are telling me that God loves me?"

I looked into her eyes, and said, "That's right. I know this for certain. God loves you. You want to know how I know? God got up on a cross and said, 'This is how much I love you.'" She paused for a moment and tears began rolling down her cheeks. Then she said, "Well, if God loves me, then nothing else matters. If God loves me, that's all that matters."

Deep down you know there are people all around you who need the love, forgiveness, grace, power, strength and comfort of God in Jesus Christ. Give me one good reason why you wouldn't want to share it?

Amen.

Do You Believe In Jesus?

For years, *TIME* magazine has named a "Person of The Year" on its January cover. In 2013, the editors of *TIME* decided to go for the doozie and name the most significant person in history. They did an exhaustive analysis ranking historical figures like Google ranks web pages. Guess who won? Jesus. And it wasn't even close (Rick Lawrence, *The Jesus Centered Life*, Group Publishing, 2016, Kindle version).

Jesus' influence on the world is staggering.

Yet, do we really know who Jesus was? Do we really know? I remember the first time I saw a picture of Jesus. I was just a little boy in Sunday school drinking grape Kool Aid and eating graham crackers. On the wall of the classroom was a sweet picture of Jesus with children all around him. He was smiling and looked like the nicest man in the universe. He looked like a divine Mister Rogers or Captain Kangaroo. He taught us to be kind to one another and love everyone. I was comforted by the picture.

Yet as I got older, I began to wonder: Why would a man who taught others to be kind to one another get brutally executed?

Whenever my Sunday school teachers talked about Jesus, they would also teach about being careful of the people you hang out with. They would talk about respecting those in authority. Yet Jesus befriended social misfits and outcasts. He hung out with people most of us would not be caught dead with. He was accused by the religious establishment of being a party animal and hanging out with riff raff. When Jesus got angry it was almost always at religious people. Jesus is usually associated with people who follow the rules and play it safe, yet he didn't do either!

Many of us believe in Jesus, but what do we believe about him — and why should it make any difference to us? What difference should it make that a man lived two thousand years ago in a place called Galilee? Can't we see him as just a great teacher and figure of history and be on our way? Or should he mean more than that? Well, according to the gospel writers and 2,000 years of Christian history and tradition

Jesus should make all the difference in the world. He should make all the difference to our lives.

What you are going to find is that when you really study Jesus, who he was, what he taught, and what he did, you are faced with a question — a very profound and penetrating question. And how you answer this question will determine your destiny as a human being. Your answer to this question will determine how you live, how you work, how you relate to the people you love and the people you hate. Your answer to this question will determine the direction of your life and the quality of your life. Your answer to this question will determine whether or not your life counts for something. Your answer to this question will determine the way you see yourself, others and the world.

To get to this question I want us to take a hard look at what Jesus said about himself. If we want to get to the real truth about Jesus, it would be a good idea to move away for a moment from what history and culture say about him and look at what he said about himself.

In John 10:30-33 Jesus makes an astonishing claim:

> *"The Father and I are one." The Jews took up stones again to stone him. Jesus replied, "I have shown you many good works from the Father. For which of these are you going to stone me?" The Jews answered, "It is not for a good work that we are going to stone you, but for blasphemy, because you, though only a human being, are making yourself God."*

Over and over again, *Jesus claimed he was God.* No other religious figure in history claimed this. Buddha, Krishna, Gandhi and Mohammed never made that claim. Only Jesus claimed to be God. Any person who makes such a claim is either nuts or telling the truth!

Let's look at another astonishing claim of Jesus in Luke 5:

> *When he saw their faith, he said, "Friend, your sins are forgiven you." Then the scribes and the Pharisees began to question, "Who is this who is speaking blasphemies? Who can forgive sins but God alone?"*

In addition to claiming he was God we see that *Jesus claimed to forgive sins.* He claimed to have the power to wipe away all those things in life that put us in the dark, that make us bitter and unable to experience joy. He claimed to have the power to set us free from those things in life that enslave us.

Have you ever known or heard of anyone who claimed to do that? I can make you more money… sure. I can get you a better job…sure. I can help you drive a better car… sure. But have you ever heard anyone tell you they can wipe away all your guilt and all your shame and all your sin, give you a fresh start and make you whole? Only Jesus made that claim.

Have you ever wanted a second chance? Have you ever wanted a new beginning? Have you ever wanted to turn your life around? Jesus claimed to have the power to give you a fresh start.

Let's look at another astonishing claim from Jesus. Most of you know this one by heart — John 3:16:

> *"For God so loved the world that he gave his only Son, so that everyone who believes in him may not perish but may have eternal life."*

Jesus claimed that if we believe in him, surrender to him, put our trust him, give our life to him and follow him, *he will give us eternal life* — a quality of life with God that begins now and is eternal in its duration! Jesus claimed that he could give us power over death! Jesus claimed that he could give us power to live forever with him and there will be no more sin, pain, violence, tears, discouragement, depression, or disease.

Have you ever feared death? Have you ever wondered what is on the other side? Have you ever longed to live in a world that has been healed? Have you ever yearned to have a body that is no longer in pain? Jesus claimed that if we follow him we don't have to fear death. It is simply the threshold to a glorious life with him forever.

Jesus claimed to be God, to forgive sins, and to give people eternal life. You see, when we truly see who Jesus claimed he was we are forced to make a decision about him. The life of Jesus demands a response. You can't read about the life of Jesus and simply say he was a great teacher or a notable figure in history. You don't have that choice. Great teachers of history don't make the claims that Jesus made. Any person who claims what Jesus claimed is either a lunatic or they are telling the truth. For example, in our assigned text in John 17, Jesus prayed about how he had revealed God to the world! He either did it or he was crazy.

So the pivotal question for each one of us is *"Who is Jesus to YOU?"* Not who is Jesus to your grandmother, mother, father, or friends, but who is Jesus to you? Is he insane or is he God? Is he crazy or is he Savior? Is he nuts or is he Lord of lords? Those are the only two choices we have.

Who is Jesus to you? How you answer that question will determine your destiny, your choices, your purpose, the quality of your life and relationships, your joy and how you view death and dying. You see, the question is personal. Very personal. It's about whether or not you want Jesus to forgive you and fill you with hope, life and joy. It's about whether or not you want a relationship with Jesus that will strengthen, encourage and sustain you the rest of your life. Who is Jesus to you? Crazy or Savior?

But you see this question is not only personal, it is communal. It's an essential question that the church needs to ask again. Because right now the American church is in crisis because we have forgotten who Jesus is and what it means to follow him. Walter Brueggemann said that "the crisis in the American church has almost nothing to with being liberal or conservative. It has everything to do with forgetting our identity as followers of Christ."

Folks, it doesn't matter if you are liberal or conservative, republican or democrat. It doesn't matter if you voted for Trump or Biden. It doesn't matter if you are a United Methodist, Baptist, or Roman Catholic. It doesn't matter whether you read from the King James Bible or the Living Bible. It doesn't matter whether you prefer 9am service or the 11am service. What matters is what you believe about Jesus Christ because Jesus is the great hope of the world!

Who is Jesus to you? Is he your one and only hope?

Maybe you are saying, "Well, I believe in God." That is not enough. What kind of God do you believe in? You see, this is why didn't we begin this series with our belief in God. We must define and know the character of the God we believe in. And we do that by understanding the person of Jesus Christ.

Colossians says that "Christ is the image of the invisible God." John 1:14 proclaims, *"And the Word became flesh and dwelt among us."* Only the Christian faith makes that claim about God — God became one of us to save us and to be in relationship with us. On our own we could never understand who God is. On our own we could never save ourselves. This is why God came to us in Jesus. This is why we believe in Jesus Christ.

We must remember what Peter Kreeft told his class at Boston University, "Christ changed every human being he ever met." If people claim to have met Jesus without being changed, they have not met Jesus. When you touch Jesus, you touch lightning."

Perhaps you feel your heart being opened today. You have tried everything else life has to offer and it has never satisfied. You've been there, done that, and have thrown away the t-shirt! Maybe you are ready to put your hope in Christ.

Rick Lawrence is a Christian ministry guru. He has written best-selling books and travels the globe leading conferences, seminars and workshops on how to grow churches and do ministry effectively. In his book "A Jesus-Centered Life" Lawrence wrote about a day when he was leading a workshop for ministry leaders and pastors. He felt depressed and worn out. He was bored with the strategies he was teaching, so he decided to throw away his notes and ask those in the workshop to talk about how Jesus was active in their lives. He said that for the next two hours the room was electric with the presence of Jesus. He had never felt more passionate about a workshop before.

After the workshop Lawrence attended other workshops and became depressed again. He felt terrible and could not put his finger on it. He found a big comfy chair in the middle of the conference arena and as he sat there watching people walk by with their notes, books, and resources, he prayed, "Lord Jesus, why do I feel this way? Why do I feel so terrible?" Lawrence said that he heard Jesus' voice almost audibly reply, "Because you are bored with everything but me now" (Lawrence, *The Jesus Centered Life*).

There are not enough golf courses, football games, and trips to the lake that can give you what Jesus Christ can give you. Only Jesus can truly satisfy and bring you home. So, who is Jesus to you? Your answer will make all the difference to your life.

If you desire to accept and receive Jesus Christ as your Lord and Savior, simply pray, Lord, I surrender my life to you. Please forgive me of my sins, fill me with your Holy Spirit, and guide me by your grace to live a life that is pleasing to you.

Amen.

Day of Pentecost
John 14:8-17 (25-27)

We Believe In The Holy Spirit

Happy Birthday, Church!

Today is Pentecost Sunday, the birthday of the church. Today we celebrate the day the Holy Spirit descended upon the church fifty days after Easter. Pentecost means fifty. Jesus promised the Spirit would come and it certainly did. The Spirit empowered the early church and Christian faith spread like wildfire. The same spirit that raised Christ from the dead and blew the church wide open lives in you! In the middle of the Apostles' Creed we say "We believe in the Holy Spirit." Ephesians underscores the importance of the Holy Spirit:

> When you believed, you were marked in him with a seal, the promised Holy Spirit, who is a deposit guaranteeing our inheritance until the redemption of those who are God's possession—to the praise of his glory. – Ephesians 1:13-14

The Holy Spirit is the spirit of God that lives inside those who follow Christ. It was the Holy Spirit that motivates you to get out of bed on Sunday morning and go to worship. It is the Holy Spirit that inspires you to serve and love others. It is the Holy Spirit that guides you to make wise decisions. And it is the Holy Spirit who convicts you when you need to change. The Holy Spirit is God's very presence inside of you, moving you, guiding you and shaping you.

But here is my question for today: How do we know the Holy Spirit is guiding us? How are we supposed to know when we are being motivated by the Spirit and not something else? How do we know when it is God who is trying to speak to us and not another impulse inside us? There are a lot of voices inside and outside of us clamoring for our attention. How do we know which one is the Holy Spirit?

I remember studying John 10 with a group of youth. We got to the part when Jesus said, "The sheep follow him because they know his voice." This young man raised his hand and said, "Pastor, I pray to

Jesus all the time but he never talks back. How am I supposed to know his voice when he never talks to me?"

Have you ever wondered what the Holy Spirit's voice sounds like? James Earl Jones? Alexa of Google? Or does it sound more like the woman's voice on your smart phone's GPS system?

Well, the truth is if we are literally hearing audible voices we probably need to take a trip to the psychiatrist, not the sanctuary. I am not saying it's impossible to hear an audible voice, but God doesn't usually operate like that. Instead, God, through the Holy Spirit, speaks to us through passion, desire, instinct, conviction and circumstance. To say we are hearing the Spirit's voice means we are being moved by the Spirit in some way.

But, again, how are we supposed to know we are being moved by the Holy Spirit? There have been times in my life when I have been faced with a decision or desired guidance. When I made my decision or chose my path I thought I was being guided by the Spirit but I was not. The whole thing blew up in my face. I prayed about it. Read scripture. I felt great about it. I did all the right things, but it was clear I made the wrong decision. I thought, "What did I miss? Where did I go wrong?"

Ever been there? Ever been confident that the decision you made was the right one, the one the Spirit was guiding you to make, and then disaster hit and all signs pointed to a bad decision?

Maybe you are faced with a decision today and you need some kind of guidance. You're seeking some sign of the Spirit, some nudge in the right direction but you are not really sure how you will know when it is the Holy Spirit guiding you. Or maybe you have made a decision and you want evidence from God that it was the right decision but you don't know what to look for.

I am going to reveal how you can be sure 99% of the time that the Holy Spirit is guiding you. I am going to show you how you can be sure whether or not the decision that you made was the right one. I am going to show you how you can confidently know you are being moved by the Holy Spirit.

I discovered something huge along my journey about how the Holy Spirit works. Through trial and error, reading scripture, listening to wise counsel I learned the key to knowing when I am going in the direction of the Holy Spirit. This key has helped me avoid a lot of mistakes. Learning this key will help you avoid a lot of mistakes too! More importantly it will help you find God's path for you.

To help us discover this key I want us to take a look at something Jesus said to his disciples about the Holy Spirit. These words appear in chapter 14 of John. Jesus was comforting his disciples in the Upper Room. They knew something bad was going to happen. Jesus was trying to break the news to them that he was going away and he was trying to comfort and encourage them. Jesus said something in the midst of his comforting sermon that I think is one of the most outrageous things he ever said. Take a look:

> *"Very truly I tell you, whoever believes in me will do the works I have been doing, and they will do even greater things than these, because I am going to the Father." — John 14:12*

The first time I saw that I thought, "Whoa! Do greater works than Jesus? What is he talking about? Jesus healed the sick, walked on water, made the blind to see, and raised the dead! How in the world can any of us do greater works than Jesus?"

What is even more confusing are these words: "Because I am going to the Father." I am sure the disciples were thinking the same thing that I was thinking. "Wait, don't we need Jesus to do all of these amazing things? How can we do great things if he is leaving us? That doesn't make any sense." Jesus brings some clarity by saying this:

> *"If you love me, keep my commands. And I will ask the Father, and he will give you another advocate to help you and be with you forever—the Spirit of truth." – John 14:15-17*

Here Jesus is introducing the Holy Spirit. This is when the light bulb went on for me. We are able to do greater works than Jesus because when Jesus ascended to the Father his Spirit began to live in each of his followers. That meant Jesus' power and influence multiplied and multiplied throughout the earth. When you compare all the work the church has done over the last 2,000 years to Jesus' three-year earthly ministry, Jesus' work was much greater.

Jesus used some interesting words to describe the Holy Spirit. Jesus called the Spirit an "advocate." The Greek word was used to describe a witness who was called in to support your case in a court of law. Or it could also be used to describe a lawyer who pleads your case when you have been charged with a serious crime. An advocate was also used to describe someone who motivated athletes who were discouraged or fatigued. Jesus also referred to the Holy Spirit as the "Spirit of Truth" because the Spirit guides us into truth and reminds us what Jesus taught. Later Jesus describes the Spirit like spring water that flows within us.

But how are we supposed to know that what is bubbling up inside of us is the Holy Spirit and not something else? How do we recognize the Spirit when we need to make decisions, find wisdom, or be guided through difficulty? Well take a look at what Jesus said next:

> "The world cannot accept him, because it neither sees him nor knows him. But you know him, for he lives with you and will be in you." – John 14:17

Jesus was saying that the world, those who live as if there was no God, can't recognize the Spirit because they interpret everything that happens out of their own ability. But Jesus' followers know him because he will be with them and in them. In other words, the difference between us and the world is that we see things based on what God is able to do through us.

We recognize the Holy Spirit's work by its ability, not our own. When I made this conclusion these words from Jesus just a few verses later popped out at me:

> "Apart from me you can do nothing." – John 15:5

Here is what I figured out: *When you find ability beyond you the Spirit is with you.*

This is the key to being sure the Spirit is moving in your life. This is the key to knowing when the Holy Spirit is guiding you. When you find power beyond you, the spirit is with you. When you find wisdom beyond you, the spirit is with you. When you know you could not have accomplished something on your own, you can be sure it was the Holy Spirit. When you have been led to a place you would have never found on your own, you can be sure it was the Holy Spirit. When you found strength to do something that seemed impossible, you can be sure it was the Holy Spirit. When you are attempting to do something that requires God's help to get it done, you can be sure you are in the right place!

The problem is too many of us are trying to do things without asking for help. We want to be in control, and so God's Spirit says, "Okay, it's all yours." And we struggle and struggle.

This may be the missing piece in your life as a Christian. Maybe you are not finding the strength or wisdom you seek because you have not activated the Holy Spirit that lives within you. Every follower of Christ has the Spirit of God within them. John Wesley believed that even nonbelievers have the Spirit of God inside them but it lies dormant. We must give the Holy Spirit permission to work.

When was the last time you activated the Spirit within you? What are you attempting right now that only the Holy Spirit could accomplish through you? What are you doing right now that you know without God would lead to utter failure?" If we are not living our faith in this way we are missing out on one of the great joys of being a follower of Christ.

The church needs this message too. If the church is not relying on the Holy Spirit we are not a church. We are an entertainment center or just another charity, but we are not a church. Being open to the movement of Spirit is essential to being a healthy and thriving church. A church can survive for a time on a good band or choir, a motivational speaker and a Facebook page but without the work of the Holy Spirit a church cannot sustain itself. It cannot be the vessel God calls it to be. Charles Spurgeon said, "Without the Spirit of God, we can do nothing. We are as ships without the wind, branches without sap, and like coals without fire, we are useless."

Unfortunately, too many churches try to do ministry without the aid of the Holy Spirit. And then they wonder why they never grow. We are good at putting a governor on the Spirit of God. We have become rather skilled at stifling the Spirit when it doesn't line up with our whims and fancies or it threatens to inconvenience us. The Spirit is strong, but it doesn't force itself on anyone or any church, so it will go only as far as we allow it.

I know of a pastor who didn't like the direction the church was going. He felt it didn't have much life. It wasn't doing the things that a church ought to be doing. It wasn't praying enough and serving enough. It wasn't studying the Bible enough. So he, led by the Spirit, started all of these small groups in the church. Lo and behold, they started to catch on, got all fired up, started to change things and shake things up. The leader of this crew started to speak all across town. He lifted up the gospel and all these people listened to him and responded. They received Christ. He was the talk of the town. Well, his church was none too pleased with all this excitement and exuberance, with all this change. They got annoyed with this group in the church and their leader. So, what did the church do? They wouldn't allow him to speak in worship anymore. His name? John Wesley. The group? Methodists!

Did you know that in the Bible the Hebrew and Greek word for Spirit literally means "wind"? Jesus said it is like a mystery, the wind. You don't see the wind, and yet you know when it comes and when it goes.

When the wind of the spirit is blowing it is an exhilarating and powerful thing. When the wind is with you there is no greater experience. I know the wind is blowing with me when someone comes up to me and says, "Your message changed my life." That was the Holy Spirit. I have the task of preaching to so many different people. How can one message meet the needs of so many? Not by my power, but by the power of the Holy Spirit. I know the wind is blowing with me when I think of someone and call them and they say, "I was just about to call you. Do you have time to talk?" I know the wind is blowing with me when I feel a nudge to text someone and they reply, "Perfect timing. I need your prayers right now." I know the wind is blowing with me when I must rely on God's power to accomplish what is before me.

Are you looking for the wind of the Spirit in your life? Pray: Lord, help me to see the evidence of you at work in my life and where it is pointing me. Open my eyes to see your hand in my life. May I sense where you are working beyond me and trust that is where you are guiding me.

When you find ability beyond you the Spirit is with you.

I used to love looking at this big palm tree on a golf course. Every time I passed it I would admire it. Then one day I passed it and it had fallen to the ground. I was upset and said, "I wonder what caused that?" And someone said, "The wind."

I once knew a man who hated the church. He told everybody he didn't believe in God. He said that religion was for weak people who couldn't stand on their own two feet. Then one day all that hardness crumbled to the ground. His heart was changed. He started going to church and he never stopped going. I don't know what happened! Someone said, "It's the wind."

There I was sixteen years old, minding my own business. I was playing tennis, getting crushes on girls, telling jokes, having fun. I was sitting in church with my parents and sisters. We were passing the mints, playing tic tac toe, and writing notes about where we wanted to go to lunch. Then this man got up to preach. I had never heard anyone like him before. I was inspired. Next thing I know I am shaking his hand at the back door of the church telling him I want to be a preacher! Me, a preacher? What happened? What caused that? You know what I think it was? The wind.

When you find ability beyond you, the Spirit is with you.

Amen.

www.ingramcontent.com/pod-product-compliance
Lightning Source LLC
Chambersburg PA
CBHW021507090426
42739CB00007B/506